MONTGOMERY AND THE BLACK MAN

Andrew Boyd

Montgomery and the Black Man

RELIGION AND POLITICS IN NINETEENTH-CENTURY ULSTER

the columba press

First published in 2006 by
the columba press
55A Spruce Avenue, Stillorgan Industrial Park,
Blackrock, Co Dublin

Cover by Bill Bolger
Origination by The Columba Press
Printed in Ireland by Betaprint, Dublin

ISBN 1 85607 517 6

The evangelicals were headed by Rev Dr Henry Cooke, a brilliant orator, a militant tory, and a natural demagogue. Opposed to Cooke's evangelical group was the new light (or 'arian') party headed by Rev Dr Henry Montgomery, a much loved and intelligent gentleman whose dignified speeches were no match for the sledge-hammer attacks of Dr Cooke.

– Donald H Akenson: *The Irish Education Experiment* (London/Toronto 1970)

Introduction

On Sunday 27 March 1966 in Dunmurry (Co Antrim) Non-Subscribing Presbyterian Church Rev William McMillan gave a lecture to commemorate the 100th anniversary of the death of Henry Montgomery. Montgomery had been minister in Dunmurry from September 1809 until December 1865.

In 1966 I was working on *Holy War in Belfast* and already knew that Montgomery and his formidable antagonist Henry Cooke had each contributed – Cooke, of course, much more effectively than Montgomery – to what would be the enduring and unchanging politics of the Protestant community in Ulster.

Cooke was a Conservative, a conformist, a strict and uncompromising Calvinist, a hero in the eyes of the Orangemen, a good friend to the Tory aristocracy. Montgomery was immeasurably more tolerant, in politics and in religion. When Cooke declared that the ministers of the Presbyterian Church should all 'wear the same livery', by which he meant they should all conform to the one creed, Montgomery's reply was that he hated livery. Livery, he said, was the badge of subjection in men … the livery of sects created as much disturbance as the livery of political parties.

In 1972 the BBC broadcast my radio documentary 'Montgomery and the Black Man' – hence the title of this book. But that brought the story no further than 1829, the year in which, tired of prolonged conflict, argument and acrimony, Montgomery and his friends withdrew from the Synod of Ulster, the governing council of the Presbyterian Church, and established the Remonstrant Synod of Ulster. I now take the story further.

But is it a story worth telling? Rev Ernest Rea, Head of

Religious Programmes in the BBC, observed more than twenty years ago that interest in Montgomery and Cooke and in the principles and doctrines about which they differed had 'not diminished with the passing of time'. Let us hope *Montgomery and the Black Man* helps to maintain that interest.

Before I conclude this brief introduction I should like to express my gratitude to Professor R Finlay Holmes, author of *Henry Cooke*; Dr E R Norman, author of *Anti-Catholicism in Victorian England*; Professor Gearóid Ó Tuathaigh, author of *Ireland Before the Famine*, and Rev Dr Ambrose Macauley for so kindly granting me permission to quote from what they have written about the times and circumstances of Montgomery and Cooke and the rudiments of their dispute, and to the publishers Routledge for permission to introduce *Montgomery and the Black Man* with what Professor Donald Akenson wrote about both of them in *The Irish Education Experiment*.

I am also indebted to Gerry Healey of the Linenhall Library for helping me find some rare information about Henry Montgomery, to Dónal Ó Luanaigh, Keeper of Collections in the National Library of Ireland, for reading the original script of this book and offering helpful advice and comment, to Rev Nigel Playfair for his concise account of the Irish Non-Subscribing Presbyterian Church after Montgomery, the present status of the church, and the philosophy of modern Unitarianism, and to Professor Alun Evans for assuring me that although a great many people died young during the nineteenth century some survived even into their nineties.

In that sense Cooke and Montgomery were survivors. Cooke was eighty years of age when he died; Montgomery was seventy-seven.

Finally I must confess that I could not have written *Montgomery and the Black Man* without the help of two gentlemen who lived and died a long time ago – J L Porter whose *Life and Times of Dr Henry Cooke DD, LL D* was first published in October 1871, and John A Crozier who published volume one of *The Life of the Rev H Montgomery LL D* in 1875.

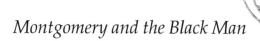

Montgomery and the Black Man

In Belfast there are two public monuments to the memory of Henry Cooke DD, LL D. One is the Cooke Centenary Church on Ormeau Road. The other is the statue, long known as the 'Black Man', at the junction of Wellington Place and College Square East, beside the College of Technology and the Royal Belfast Academical Institution. There is also a white marble portal in May Street Presbyterian church. There is no public monument to Henry Montgomery LL D. He was Cooke's contemporary and his principal opponent in several bitter and enduring controversies about religion and politics.

Cooke and Montgomery were Presbyterian clergymen, both born in 1788 and both eminent in the public life of nineteenth century Ireland. Cooke was a conformist who enjoyed the confidence and support of landowners and Orangemen, though neither a landowner nor an Orangeman himself. In matters of theology and church government he was strict and orthodox. Montgomery was more liberal. He campaigned for civil rights, free speech, Catholic Emancipation, and the reform of parliament. He also believed that the Christian churches had a duty to be tolerant and charitable to one another, irrespective of their different forms of worship.

As ten-year-old boys Cooke and Montgomery both witnessed, and in different ways long afterwards remembered, arson, terror, and public executions during the Rebellion of the United Irishmen in 1798. In Maghera, near where he was born, Cooke saw the militiamen arrest and execute known republicans, like his neighbour Watty Graham, and burn down their houses. John Glendy, his own Presbyterian minister, would

9

have been either executed or imprisoned if he had not escaped to America. What young Cooke saw then he remembered all his life. He often said it was what made him a conservative and a respecter of the established constitution.

Montgomery was different. He was not ashamed to acknowledge that some of his own 'kith and kin' had fought in '98, and that he always found his 'best and most warm-hearted friends' among the United Irishmen who had survived the rebellion. When he was a boy he saw his own home, Boltnaconnell House at Killead in South Antrim, ransacked and set on fire by the militia. They had come to arrest his two older brothers, William and John. Both were rebels who had fought in the Battle of Antrim. Fortunately, the brothers had been warned. They escaped in time.

Montgomery probably enjoyed a more comfortable childhood than Henry Cooke. His son-in-law, John A Crozier, would in later years describe Boltnaconnell House as 'a pleasant old mansion'. His father, Archibald Montgomery, was an officer in the Irish Volunteers, a gentleman farmer, a tolerant and democratic man. Cooke's father was a hard-working smallholder whom Professor J L Porter has described in the *Life and Times of Henry Cooke* as

> a plain man of little education and less pretence ... one of those industrious, independent yeomen who contributed much to the prosperity and loyalty of Ulster.

Cooke's mother, Jane Cooke, seems to have been a more assertive person. She was, according to Porter, a woman of folklore and legend, of 'romantic tales and ballads'. Her son Henry was therefore

> indebted to her for most of those anecdotes, incidents of Irish history, and scraps of ballad poetry, which in after years he recited with much pathos and power.

It was undoubtedly she who told him that one of his ancestors was no more than a baby when carried as a refugee to the City of Derry, and was there, sheltering under a cannon-gun, during the historic siege of 1689. That child and his father had escaped from 'a distant part of County Down' where all the other members of their family had been massacred. Cooke would often say that 'the God of battles protected the motherless and homeless boy'.

Jane Cooke made sure that Henry, the youngest of her four children, received as good an education as a woman in her position could in those times afford. Joseph Pollock, a strictly religious Scottish Presbyterian, was the first schoolmaster to whom he was sent. Pollock was an excellent teacher but his schoolhouse was poor and primitive. It was just a small thatched cabin, like far too many schoolhouses in eighteenth century rural Ireland.

> The seats were black oak sticks from the neighbouring bog. A fire of peat blazed, or rather smoked, in the middle of the floor, and a hole in the roof served for a chimney.

Cooke's boyhood education must have been an early form of what is known today in Northern Ireland as integrated education. Joseph Pollock respected the faith of all his young pupils individually. In his school

> catechisms were enforced without exception and without distinction. The Shorter Catechism of the Westminster Divines, the Church Catechism, and the Christian doctrines of the Roman Catholics were taught to the members of the respective sects.

Henry Cooke was obviously not taught to be bigoted, at least not in any of the early schools he attended nor indeed, it would seem, at any time during his childhood. He would not have heard bigotry preached in any of John Glendy's sermons.

Pollock was one of the several schoolmasters by whom he was educated. After a term with each of the others he finished eventually under the tuition of a classical scholar called Frank Glass, a Catholic, said also to have been a republican, who had opened a school in the village of Tobermore. Tobermore was five miles from where Cooke lived, through fields and bogs, and across the Moyola, a river which would often be in flood during the winter months and dangerous to cross even at the ford.

Glass and his pupils were moved about no less than five times in search of a proper schoolhouse. The places they tried must really have been derelict, considering, as Henry Cooke later recalled, that they finally settled in a house in which the two window-frames had been without glass for a long time and were stuffed with sods. The windows would remain like that until there was enough money to pay a glazier. There was one table but that was used exclusively by the master, who also took the only stool in the place. Young Henry Cooke at first thought the stool would be his, but he had to give it up and sit on a cold stone, like all the other boys.

Henry Montgomery was eleven years of age when he started attending classes in Isaac Patton's front parlour. Patton was an elderly clergyman who lived at Lyle Hill, four miles or so from Boltnaconnell House. But all Montgomery remembered learning, during the three years he went there, was 'the rudiments of Latin and the Shorter Catechism'. Early in 1803 he asked his parents to let him transfer to Nathaniel Alexander's school in Crumlin, a village somewhat further away from Boltnaconnell House than Lyle Hill. And that, as John A Crozier later observed, was 'a very decided change for the better'. At Crumlin Academy, which was then one of the best schools in the North of Ireland, Montgomery was settled in

> a more congenial atmosphere, with schoolfellows who, like himself
> … would afterwards become members of the ministerial, medical or
> legal professions, or farmers and country gentlemen in their several
> neighbourhoods.

Montgomery probably first heard of Arianism, a philosophy (or theology) that would later involve him in much prolonged controversy, when he was a pupil in the Crumlin Academy. Arianism was the creed of Arius, a priest in ancient Alexandria. Although asserting himself a Christian, Arius denied the divinity of Christ. His creed (or heresy) was suppressed for more than a thousand years but was revived soon after the Protestant Reformation. By the middle of the eighteenth century an appreciable number of Presbyterians in Ireland, in England and in

Scotland were Arians, some merely nominally, others more zealously. Nathaniel Alexander was an Arian. He was the Presbyterian minister in Crumlin as well as being headmaster of the academy.

* * *

Cooke and Montgomery were being educated for the Presbyterian ministry. They would both be required therefore to matriculate at the University of Glasgow and attend the pre-scribed courses of lectures. Cooke was just a 14-year-old boy in 1803 when he first made the journey to Glasgow. There was no public transport on the route. Other available forms of transport were too expensive for a young man of his very limited means. He had, therefore, to walk the whole of sixty miles from his home at Grillagh, near Maghera, to Donaghadee in County Down. From Donaghadee he sailed on the mail-packet boat to Portpatrick, and from there walked the rest of the way to Glasgow, stopping overnight at houses-of-call. Fortunately

> the Irish students were known along the route, especially on the Scotch side of the channel. Every house was open to them.

There would have been many other students from the North of Ireland going at around the same time to Glasgow. It is there-fore unlikely that young Henry Cooke would have had to travel alone. He afterwards told J L Porter that

> before the commencement of each session, groups of young men as-sembled in different parts of Ulster, and travelled together, enliven-ing the monotony of the road by anecdote, legend and sallies of native wit.

Cooke and Montgomery were not particularly impressed by the quality of the teaching in the University of Glasgow. The professors there did not seem to care how the students studied, where they lived, or what they did in or out of the classroom. Montgomery said later that in Glasgow the education of the stu-dents 'became in a great measure dependent on themselves' and that he himself felt that when there he had been 'mainly self-taught'.

Nonetheless he and Cooke followed the prescribed courses and read the subjects they were required to read as prospective candidates for the Presbyterian ministry in Ireland – theology, church history, the ancient biblical languages etc. Cooke also attended elocution classes where he did much to correct his rural Ulster accent and improve his speech and delivery. Montgomery also aspired to oratory, but was interested as well in English literature and the proper use of the English language.

Eventually they graduated or at least completed the prescribed course. They then returned home to be 'licensed' by the Presbyterian church authorities. After that they could present themselves for ordination to any congregation that judged them suitable.

In November 1808, six months after his twentieth birthday, Cooke was ordained assistant minister at Duneane, near Randalstown. But he soon showed himself to be much too serious for the easy-going Presbyterians of that part of Antrim. They did not want to be harangued every Sunday by a young, newly-qualified zealot. Robert Scott, the ageing and far from orthodox senior minister at Duneane, was said to be 'highly displeased'.

> The people [wrote J L Porter] had never heard such preaching. All were roused; some were deeply impressed; but many were indignant to be thus rudely awakened from a pleasant dream of security. Cooke was treated with coldness. His fervour was sneered at, and stigmatised as Methodism. Difficulties were thrown in his way which he was unable to overcome.

One of difficulties was the income, a meagre £25 a year. But he stayed two years at Duneane, in near starvation, wrote Porter, and resigned in November 1810. Two months later he was appointed minister to the Presbyterian congregation of Donegore, near Templepatrick. Montgomery was also a candidate for that ministry but was rejected when he confessed that he was a Unitarian, which meant the same thing as Arian, and that he thought candidates for the ministry should not be required to subscribe to the Westminster Confession of Faith, the historic creed of orthodox Presbyterians.

The Arians had their own peculiar and often varying inter-pretations of Christianity yet, as ministers individually and as congregations, they were tolerated for more than 100 years within the Presbyterian churches. Arians, or Socinians, may also have survived individually within some of the other churches but without revealing themselves. Socinianism is another form of Unitarianism. It was first preached by Fausto Paolo Sozzini (Socinus), an Italian theologian who lived, 1539-1604, during the first century of the Reformation.

The Presbyterians of Donegore, an affluent congregation, ob-viously felt they had made the safer choice when they appointed the orthodox Henry Cooke. But by a fortunate coincidence, the day of his failure at Donegore, Montgomery received an invit-ation from the congregation of Dunmurry whose minister, Andrew George Malcolm, had moved to Newry.

As it happened the Dunmurry congregation was traditionally more Unitarian than orthodox. The church elders probably did not even bother to ask Montgomery questions about the Westminister Confession. And so, when the whole congregation was canvassed on 9 July they were 'perfectly unanimous in wishing Mr Montgomery to be their minister'. He was therefore ordained at Dunmurry, at the age of twenty-one, on 14 September 1809. His stipend was to be £86 (Irish) with £50 (Irish) as his share of the *regium donum*, and a glebe of eight acres. The *regium donum* was the subsidy which the government paid to the Presbyterian clergy.

That was Montgomery's original pastoral settlement, though as time passed his income from the church, the glebe, the *regium donum*, and teaching would amount to around £600 a year. That was a substantial sum in the mid-nineteenth century, many times the average income of Presbyterian ministers. Montgomery would remain minister at Dunmurry for the rest of his life and be buried, fifty-six years later, in the churchyard there.

In October 1817, he turned down an invitation to become minister to the congregation in Killyleagh, sent to him by

Archibald Hamilton Rowan, a famous figure in the late Society of United Irishmen. The previous minister, William D McEwen, had left Killyleagh in April to take care of a congregation in Belfast.

Hamilton Rowan was a Unitarian and knew that Montgomery, 'a gentleman of whose liberal opinions and excellent character [he had heard] so much praise', was of the same persuasion. He must have been impressed by reports of Montgomery's spirited defence of William Steel Dickson at the annual meeting of the Synod of Ulster earlier that year, and by his speech in 1813 when the Synod passed a resolution supporting equal rights for the Catholics.

Steel Dickson was one of the Presbyterian clergymen imprisoned after the '98 Rebellion. Because of his political opinions he was still being persecuted, fifteen years after the defeat of the rebels, by certain influential and well-connected members of the Synod, notably by Robert Black, the minister in Derry. Dr Black was the almoner or agent appointed by the government to control and distribute the *Regium Donum*. He was a friend and confidant of Lord Castlereagh, architect of the Act of Union and exterminator of the United Irishmen.

Montgomery had good reasons, personal and professional, for not wanting to move to Killyleagh. He was awaiting confirmation of his appointment as head master of the English department in the Belfast Academical Institution. The appointment was confirmed a week or ten days after he received Hamilton Rowan's first letter. He of course accepted the position. It was what he wanted. With the approval of his congregation he would remain pastor of Dunmurry and continue, for the following twenty-two years, to be Head Master of English in the Academical Institution.

A few months later, upon the recommendation of William McEwen, the congregation of Killyleagh invited Henry Cooke to deliver a sermon, that usually being preliminary to appointment as pastor. McEwen was a Unitarian but at that time had a high opinion of Henry Cooke, a young man who had not yet publicly expressed what would soon be his marked and sustained hostil-ity to the Unitarians. McEwen did, in fact, send the following letter to one of the elders in Killyleagh.

> ... By rendering every service in your power to Mr Cooke, you will secure to yourself the society of a well-informed man, and to the congregation a useful and popular preacher. He is by no means big-oted in his opinions, and has too much good sense not to be charita-ble towards those who differ from him in sentiment ... He possess-es great general information, and you will find him a good scholar, an able preacher, and an honourable man.

During the eight years he was the minister of Donegore, Cooke had been given generous leave of absence, first to return to Glasgow University to complete his theological studies, and later to enrol for certain courses at Trinity College Dublin. In both those universities he studied medicine and anatomy, as well as theology, philosophy, the sacred scriptures, and the other subjects that clergymen in all churches normally study. He was therefore an immeasurably more learned man when he went to Killyleagh than he had been when appointed minister at Donegore, but he was still strictly orthodox, still committed to the Westminster Confession of Faith and to the Trinitarian inter-pretation. He was inaugurated minister of Killyleagh on 8 September 1818.

* * *

Among the elders by whom he was most warmly welcomed was Captain Sydney Hamilton Rowan, the younger son of Archibald Hamilton Rowan. Sydney Hamilton Rowan was also a Conservative in politics and orthodox in religion.

> He was a man of sound judgement [wrote J L Porter], extensive theological knowledge, refined taste, ardent piety and undaunted courage ... animated by love for evangelical truth and by the desire to eradicate Arianism from the Presbyterian Church in Ireland ... In him Cooke found that sympathy and encouragement of which he had been so long in search.

Arius of Alexandria began preaching his particular doctrine at a time when the Emperor Constantine the Great had estab-

lished Christianity as the recognised state religion that would
replace the old pagan gods and unite the people of the Roman
Empire in one faith. Arius was now raising doubts and threatening to cause divisions and disruption. His doctrine was condemned by the Council of Nicea and declared a heresy in AD
325.

Arius's interpretation of Christianity prevails nonetheless to
the present day. There are Arians (or Unitarians) all over the
world. As recently as 19 October 2003, to quote only one of what
universally must be countless Unitarian parsons, the Reverend
Christine Robinson of the First Unitarian Church in Albuquerue,
New Mexico, stated that

> Bishop Arius disagreed heartily with the notion that Jesus had been
> or was God, for a reason that seemed obvious to him: Jesus had
> been a person, walking the earth, eating, drinking and doing all
> sorts of other things completely unbefitting divinity. Arius argued
> well and he had many followers but he lost his battle. His views,
> which he thought of as Unitarian, were finally denounced by the
> Church and Trinitarianism became orthodoxy.

Montgomery's ten-page definition of the Unitarian theology,
The Creed of an Arian, is not quite so simple as Christine
Robinson's. Writing in 1830 he rejected all 'man-made' theology,
such as the Westminster Confession of Faith and, relying upon
his own private judgement and interpretation, accepted only
what was written in the Bible – nothing else.*

In the days of Montgomery and Henry Cooke the
Westminster Confession of Faith defined Trinitarianism, the
Holy Trinity, as

> … three persons in the Godhead, the Father, the Son and the Holy
> Ghost, and these three are one God, the same in substance, equal in
> power and glory.

Arianism or the Holy Trinity, Unitarianism or Trinitarianism, would be the doctrines upon which Henry Cooke and
his followers would argue and campaign until, fifteen centuries
after the Council of Nicea had purged the Roman Church, they

---

* Crozier, *Life of Rev Henry Montgomery LL D* (Appendix F)

had purged Irish Presbyterianism of the same heresy and had compelled all ministers, candidates for the ministry, and young men studying to be ministers unconditionally to accept and sign the Westminster Confession of Faith.

Their campaign began in the spring of 1821 when it was announced in the Belfast newspapers that the Reverend John Smethurst, of Exeter, had been appointed by the English Unitarian Fund to visit the Province of Ulster, and would shortly commence his mission by preaching in Belfast, Carrickfergus, Lisburn, Saintfield, Downpatrick, Killyleagh, and adjoining districts.

It would seem from the wording of the press advertisements that it was the English Unitarians who had sent Smethurst to Ulster, probably at the request of the Presbytery of Antrim, which had always been Arian, and of certain professors teaching in the Belfast Academical Institution.

Having assured all who were interested that he would 'advocate the cause of Christian truth without any reference to sect or party', Smethurst was invited to preach even in the parishes of orthodox ministers. But once there, according to J L Porter,

> he assailed the doctrine of the Trinity, insulted the Trinitarians, told them they taught the supreme Deity of the Saviour because they lived by it, and generally concluded his address with a few political touches advocating advanced liberal views, which most thoughtful men would call revolutionary.

Nonetheless, Smethurst's oratory, his 'free theology and still freer political creed' attracted great numbers of people, particularly those who still remembered the heroic rebels of '98. The English Unitarians, the Presbyters of Antrim, and the professors in the Belfast Academical Institution might thus have seen the great results they expected had Smethurst not gone to Killyleagh. He was invited there by Archibald Hamilton Rowan.

When Smethurst addressed the meeting in Killyleagh, Henry Cooke and Sydney Hamilton Rowan were also present, to tell him he was a heretic and that his heresies would be answered the following Sunday. He and his friends would be welcome if they cared to come and listen.

Smethurst did not come, but when the news of Cooke's challenge got out Killyleagh Presbyterian Church was packed to overflowing that Sunday. People had come from far and near to hear how Henry Cooke would denounce the unfortunate Smethurst and expound the true gospel of Jesus Christ. Those who were unable to get into the church 'clustered round the doors and windows'. It was then that Cooke's prolonged campaign against the Unitarians really started.

After the meetings at Killyleagh, Cooke and Sydney Hamilton Rowan turned up wherever Smethurst would be preaching – Saintfield, Downpatrick, Carrickfergus, or any other place where he was billed to be. Cooke interrupted Smethurst, put questions, contradicted the Arian theology, and expounded what he believed to be the truth. That continued until Smethurst decided he had had enough of 'that gentleman from Killyleagh who appeared to be most dreadfully alarmed about Unitarianism'. He brought his mission to a close and returned to England.

By then, according to J L Porter, 'Cooke was recognised throughout Ulster as the champion of Bible truth.' Porter could also have added, as Professor R Finlay Holmes was to observe more than 150 years later, that

> Cooke had now tasted the excitement of public controversy and the heady wine of popular acclaim and he was to remain an addict for the remainder of his life. Almost by accident he had stumbled upon a way of reaching and influencing public opinion …

Furthermore, if Smethurst's political opinions were so liberal as to be almost revolutionary, Cooke could now appeal to the conservative opposite – respect for the status quo, respect for the rulers of states, respect for established authority in church and state. And so, Professor Holmes has concluded,

> the Smethurst episode established both the foundations of Cooke's popularity and the essentials of his creed.

Having dealt to his satisfaction with Smethurst, Cooke turned his attention to what he feared was ' another stronghold of Arianism', the Belfast Academical Institution where Henry Montgomery, an avowed Unitarian, was head master of the English department. When, in 1821, William Bruce, another Arian, was appointed professor of the Biblical languages, Hebrew and Greek, Cooke decided he must act. At the 1822 annual meeting of the Synod in Newry he called 'special attention' to the appointment of Bruce, reminded his colleagues that some of the students at the institution were being trained to enter the Presbyterian minister, and then

> warned his brethren and the whole church of the danger of permitting a man professing Arian views, however high his qualifications in other respects, to instruct candidates for the ministry.

William Bruce was the son, grandson, great grandson etc. of six generations of Presbyterian ministers, going back to Michael Bruce (1635-93). His father, also William Bruce, had been an officer in the Irish Volunteers and was known often to have preached in the pulpit wearing the uniform of Lisburn True Blues – short blue swallow-tail coat with red cuffs, white breeches, black top-boots. Besides being minister of Belfast First congregation, Bruce Senior was also principal of Belfast Academy, a position which did not endear him to the board of the rival Belfast Academical Institution nor they to him. And for that reason, despite Henry Cooke's fear of Arian influence, a majority on the board of the institution, including the Unitarians, were hostile when the younger William Bruce's application was considered. He was nonetheless appointed after efforts on his behalf by Sir Robert Bateson, representing the Church of Ireland, and Robert Reid, Moderator that year of the Presbyterian Synod of Ulster.

Cooke spoke at some length about the appointment of Bruce. He expounded his own orthodox opinions, quoted scripture, and denounced all Unitarians as the enemies of truth. His speech, however, made no impression, neither on the Unitarians present nor on those of the orthodox opinion. As the Orthodox and the Unitarians had tolerated one another for as long as anyone could remember, Cooke's attack, particularly his hostility to the Belfast Academic Institution, was then altogether out of place.

Nonetheless, the Arian controversy had now become his 'one absorbing thought'. He returned home from Newry to have nightmares and midnight hallucinations in which he imagined he was pursued by John Smethurst, Henry Montgomery, William Bruce and other Arians, and in which he saw the devil as a Unitarian trying to convince him that Jesus Christ was not God. When, in response to that outrageous assertion, Cooke called the devil 'a liar and the father of lies' the words were 'uttered with such strength of voice and vehemence of action' that he startled his wife. She woke up thinking burglars had broken in.

In 1823 the Belfast Academical Institution was again discussed at the annual meeting of the Synod, but the debate ended indecisively and was not even recorded in the minutes. By then, being convinced that his colleagues in the ministry showed 'no wish to grapple with the Arian heresy', Cooke decided to put his case to the Presbyterian laity who, he felt, would be eager to hear 'the pure gospel doctrine'.

* * *

So he set out on journeys to many different places, travelling often long distances on foot and on horseback and addressing two and sometimes three meetings every week. There can be no doubt that he attracted audiences wherever he went for even those who disagreed most with his theology and his politics acknowledged that his demeanour and personal appearance – tall, spare and slight, with erect carriage – and his skill in the pulpit and on the public platform made him 'one of the most powerful and popular speakers'. Crozier agreed that when addressing public meetings or congregations assembled for worship Cooke had

> unfailing command of language and often strikingly quaint, figurative and attractive turns of thought and expression, amazing powers of humorous sarcasm and impassioned denunciation, infinite quickness in reply, a most thorough knowledge of the feelings, expectations, and wishes of his auditory, graceful and telling elocution.

Cooke was described in an English publication *The Athenaeum* as

... a platform orator of a very superior type [who] could easily carry away an ignorant or half-educated assembly, causing them to weep or laugh as he pleased.

Montgomery, for his part, 'cheerfully admitted' that he found Cooke 'an open and manly opponent, usually frank and fearless but not always very scrupulous about means and weapons when in a difficulty'.

Oratory is, of course, a very special skill, perhaps an art. Speeches and sermons have to be carefully prepared, or at least well thought out, before delivery. Some orators need notes and some speak well from memory. It is obvious that Cooke and Montgomery did prepare their speeches most carefully, and deliver them each in a particular and individual style.

Montgomery's own style has been described as 'graceful, chaste and classic' and his voice 'singularly sweet'. J L Porter thought his defence of the Unitarians at the synod assembly in 1828 an unsurpassed and 'wonderful display of oratory, wit, pathos and powerful declamation'. Perhaps the effect was further enhanced by the appearance of the orator. Montgomery was a tall, heavily-built man, standing six-feet-three-inches in height, and always immaculately dressed.

* * *

As well as continuing his personal campaign against the Unitarians in Ulster and elsewhere, Cooke took up the cause of the scattered Presbyterian communities and families in the south and west of Ireland, travelling to Scotland to raise funds on their behalf and to enlist the goodwill and aid of the Scottish church. Back home he quietly organised a group of friends and supporters upon whom he could rely when, once again, he would ask the Synod of Ulster to oppose what he believed was the spreading influence of the Unitarians.

Cooke's obsession with Arianism and particularly his hostility to the Belfast Academical Institution made not only the Unitarians but also many of the orthodox ministers suspect he was becoming dangerously disruptive. That is probably why he was rejected by the congregation of Armagh when they needed a minister in the summer of 1823. J L Porter alleged in his biography of Cooke that while 'the great body of the congregation' were anxious to have Cooke as their pastor a few Unitarians in Armagh were 'just as anxious to prevent his settlement among them'. The vacancy in Armagh was later filled by P S Henry, a 'more moderate man than Cooke', but certainly not a Unitarian.*

Nonetheless Cooke's work on behalf of the Presbyterians in the south and west seems to have been appreciated. In 1824 he was elected Moderator of the Synod of Ulster. He would hold that position for one year and enjoy the consequent prestige and influence.

At that time politically articulate Catholics in Ireland, and in Britain, were demanding the same rights as all other citizens of the United Kingdom and an end to the certain forms of anti-Catholic discrimination. It was then that Sydney Smith, later to be Canon of St Paul's Cathedral in London, wrote the *Peter Plymly Letters* in defence of what would soon be known as Catholic Emancipation.

Smith asked why the English were endangering their own church and state for the sake of 'ten or twelve great Orange families' who had been 'sucking the blood' of Ireland for a hundred years and more. By 'great Orange families' he meant the ennobled Protestant landowners of Ireland, people such as the Earl of Roden, Lord Mountcashel, Lord Londonderry, and many more of that class. They were the people with whom Henry Cooke would soon be intimately associated. He and the great Orange families would stand by one another for more than forty years, resisting every reform which they feared would curtail their power, threaten their property and erode their influence.

Shortly before Cooke became Moderator, the government appointed parliamentary commissions to inquire into the state of affairs in Ireland and to advise, among other things, what

---

*P S Henry was appointed President of Queen's College (later Queen's University) in 1849.

might be done about Catholic rights, and about education at all
levels, including non-denominational education for Irish children of primary school age. As Moderator of the Presbyterian
Church in Ireland, Cooke was invited to London to give evidence to the commissioners and to both Houses of Parliament.

In November 1824 he wrote a memoir in which he explained
in detail, much from his own experience as a schoolboy, 'the
state of primary education in Ulster, the nature of the schoolhouses, the character of the teachers, and the class-books read'. J
L Porter was certain that Cooke's memoir on education

> helped to open the eyes of the Royal Commissioners to the wants of
> Ireland in regard to education … suggested the leading points on
> which information and reform were needed, and laid down princi-
> ples at once sound and suitable for the divided state of the parties
> and religious sects in Ireland.

When in London Cooke took the opportunity to speak to
MPs and peers about the Arian influence in the Belfast Academical
Institution. He also warned them that

> undue concessions to the Catholic party … would only incite to
> further demands and in the end tend to overthrow any scheme of
> united education.

When asked what Protestants in Ulster thought of Catholic
Emancipation he replied that so far as he could see opinions
were 'exceedingly varied among all classes of people'. Some
merely disliked the idea of Catholics being granted equal rights.
Some positively disapproved. There were some in favour. He
added that the better-informed Presbyterians seemed to have little
fear of the Catholics being granted their rights, within certain
limits, but that the lesser-informed almost entirely disapproved.
By the lesser-informed Cooke had in mind people who knew little
or nothing about politics and public affairs, those whom *The
Athenaeum* described as 'the ignorant and half-educated'. That
would certainly have been the majority of Ulster Protestants,
and Catholics. In this, however, he did not go as far as his friend
Lord Mountcashel who would later tell the House of Lords that

ninety-nine per cent of Presbyterians in Ireland did not want Catholics to have the same rights as Protestants.

Cooke therefore seemed, at least when he was in London, to be somewhat more tolerant than Mountcashel. He told the commissioners that personally he thought 'the admission of Catholics to equal rights' would diminish rather than increase 'certain animosities'. He did not know any Protestants who would object if equal rights meant rights of personal security, ownership of property or religious belief. But if equal rights meant admission to offices of state and positions of political authority then many Protestants would most certainly object. In a letter home he informed his wife that

> ... the committees of the two Houses are here considered as running breast high in favour of Catholic Emancipation. It will be strongly opposed but I think it will finally succeed. I have given my opinion fully in favour of limited concession but have stated a great number of Protestants are hostile – among whom I believe I might have counted yourself; but husband and wife cannot always agree.

When later challenged to substantiate his assertion that the majority of Ulster Protestants would refuse the Catholics equal rights, Cooke replied that he had been born the subject of a Protestant state which was established by his Protestant forefathers. He would continue to speak and to act in defence of the liberties he enjoyed. He therefore refused to withdraw what he had said.

Cooke's condemnation of the Belfast Academical Institution as a 'seminary of Arianism' was also published and greatly offended the management, the teachers and the students in that establishment. All of them stated, in separate but unanimous declarations, that although the institution had been founded and financed by men who had been mostly Unitarians it was nonetheless a non-sectarian establishment, 'resolutely opposed to and prohibiting any denominational or doctrinal ascendancy' whether Unitarian, Trinitarian, or of any other persuasion.

As a Unitarian and as a teacher in the institution Montgomery was one of the first to answer Cooke. He felt that his honour as a teacher, responsible for the instruction and guidance of students of all denominations, including Roman Catholics, had been 'publicly and deliberately impeached'.

The newspapers, including even the conservative and orthodox *Belfast News Letter*, also publicly rebuked Cooke and challenged his allegations. But, once again, Cooke stood up against all this criticism. In an 'elaborate pamphlet' he defended the evidence he had given to the politicians and commissioners in London, and called upon 'all loyal and orthodox men' to support him in his campaign against 'Arians, Radicals and Papists'.

> Nor did he call in vain [wrote Montgomery years later]. The entire Orangemen of Ireland, from the peer in his castle to the peasant in his hovel, rallied round him; and Orthodoxy, in all its phases, hailed him as its champion. Thus uniting Evangelicalism with Orangeism, and the countenance of the aristocracy with the applause of the multitude, in a few months from the publication of his evidence he had acquired extraordinary popularity and influence.

* * *

By now Henry Cooke was convinced that if the Unitarians were not stopped they would take over the entire Presbyterian Church in Ireland and leave no room for the Orthodox. His exact words, when he delivered that warning to the Synod of Ulster, were 'we must put down Arianism or Arianism will put us down'.

That the Unitarians were converting others within the Presbyterian Church was no secret. That was the proud boast of individuals such as William Porter, an avowed Unitarian who was also the Clerk of Synod, and of William Bruce the elder. In his biography of Cooke, J L Porter portrays these men as dogmatic and tyrannical.

> Though their doctrines had not gained ground among the people their influence in the church courts had increased to such an extent that the foundations of the faith were shaken, and the safeguards of orthodoxy all but destroyed. Timid men trembled before the frown of Porter, the eloquence of Montgomery and the polished satire of Bruce.

The same timid men would soon find comfort and assurance in the equally dogmatic rhetoric of Henry Cooke.

Many of the more liberal Irish historians, and certainly all who are of the nationalist outlook, seem to think that Cooke's religious principles camouflaged, or at least complemented, his political orthodoxy, his popularity with the Orangemen, his reliance upon the goodwill and support of the landowning aristocracy.

To what extent was that so? Was Cooke as much a bigot in politics as he was in religion? John A Crozier thought it was his 'extreme' Toryism, his hostility to the Roman Catholics and his defence of church and state that 'gathered the Orangemen of Ulster into his following'. J L Porter too admitted that his

> strong political opinions, combined with theological opinions still stronger, made him to some extent obnoxious to the majority of the people of Ireland. His opposition to the revolutionary views and dangerous agitation of O'Connell was scarcely less determined than his opposition to Arianism.

Cooke would deal later with Daniel O'Connell. His main problem in the latter half of the 1820s was how he might curtail the influence and power of the Unitarians and possibly drive them out of the church entirely. He became ill in the summer of 1826, whether from overwork, as Porter suggests, or from some other cause, and feared he was about to die. But his fear of death was unfounded. He soon recovered, whatever his ailment, under the care of his friend Dr McDowel in Dublin and after two weeks rest and recuperation in Moore Park, the home and estate of Lord Mountcashel. During those two weeks, Mountcashel convinced him that the Unitarians would have to be got rid of altogether. He returned to Belfast with that thought uppermost in his mind.

At the beginning of the next annual meeting of the Synod assembly, June 1827 in Strabane, Robert Magill, the minister in Antrim, rose to denounce the Unitarians and move that

> Mr Porter, having avowed himself an Arian before the Commissioners of Irish Education, be no longer continued as Clerk.

The building in which the Synod met was crowded that day. Thirty-eight church elders and 130 ministers were there to debate the current affairs of the Irish Presbyterian Church. The assembly had also attracted 'a vast concourse of people of all denominations', among them many Church of Ireland clergymen, with their wives and children. They had all come to listen and observe the proceedings, and many, since Strabane was a stronghold of Orangeism, to demonstrate their support for Henry Cooke who was now acclaimed 'the redoubted leader of Orthodoxy and opponent of the Roman Catholic claims'.

At first Magill's proposition attracted some support but it soon became clear that most of the assembly were surprised that he should have made so graceless a proposition. Most of the ministers and elders felt that William Porter, despite his views on the nature of Jesus Christ, had been a competent and considerate secretary for upwards of the past eleven years and should therefore be confirmed in the position he held. William Wright, the outgoing Moderator, then proposed the following amendment to Magill's motion:

> though the Synod highly disapprove and disavow Arian principles, yet as Mr Porter has always faithfully discharged his duty as Clerk he shall be retained in office.

That amendment no doubt disconcerted Cooke and his colleagues. It nonetheless gave them what they were after – a debate on the nature Unitarianism. Henry Montgomery was the first to speak. He claimed that Porter was accused not of being neglectful in his duties as Clerk of Synod but of 'having honestly professed what he believed to be the truth' when giving evidence on oath before a parliamentary commission.

The debate on Magill's proposition and the several amendments proposed continued for the best part of the next two days, during which Porter declared that he knew, on authority, that the whole affair had been planned beforehand and that he was the victim of a conspiracy in which the chief movers were Cooke himself and Robert Stewart of Broughshane, Cooke's clever friend and adviser, a man of intrigue.

As the debate continued it soon became obvious that an appreciable number of ministers and church elders did not want to punish Porter, merely because of the opinions he held on certain aspects of Christian doctrine. In the end the assembly decided, by a majority of ninety-one to thirty-two, that while deeply regretting Porter's 'avowal of Arianism' they did not consider he should thereby be dismissed from the Clerkship since that might ' be construed as persecution for the sake of opinion'.

Cooke was still not content. Next day he and his supporters asked for and were granted the right to enter a protest in the minutes of the Synod. This time forty-one ministers and fourteen elders supported him. That total was appreciably more than the number who had voted the previous day for the impeachment of Porter. But neither the recorded protest nor the greater number supporting Cooke was the end of the affair – far from it. According to Crozier, the protest and the conspiracy to remove Porter from the clerkship were 'merely skirmishing'. The real attack on the Unitarians had yet to come. It came almost immediately after Cooke had handed in the protest.

Quoting William Porter's own assertion that within the Irish Presbyterian community there were 'more real Arians than professed ones', Cooke proposed that 'to provide a public testimony to the truth' ministers and elders should affirm, orally and by signature, that they each adhered to the doctrine of the Trinity as it is defined in the Westminster Shorter Catechism.

The debate which followed continued through Thursday, Friday and Saturday. Montgomery condemned 'the folly of man-made creeds', among which he included the Westminster Confession of Faith. Cooke declared that there could be no peace where there were doctrinal divisions and no harmony 'amid the opposing elements of theological dogmas'.

At the end of the debate, when the names of all present had been read out, 117 ministers and eighteen elders, one by one, declared themselves orthodox. Eight ministers and five elders abstained, protesting that the whole procedure was contrary to the rules of the Synod. Montgomery and three others left while the names were being called. Two ministers refused to sign or affirm. With that result, wrote J L Porter, it was clear that

... Arian influence was at an end in the Synod, and that the only honourable course open to the defeated body was a speedy withdrawal. This was just what Mr Cooke wanted.

Montgomery and his three friends returned to their lodgings, disappointed and depressed. They had seen many whom they had believed to be Unitarians give their consent that day to Henry Cooke. A number of those men evidently lacked the courage to be different from the majority. Others feared rejection by their congregations, loss of income, eviction and impoverishment at a time when 'social welfare' consisted of little more than an occasional meal and an item of cast-off clothing from one of the few charities that then helped the poor. At that time the average income of a Presbyterian minister was £100 to £150 per year. That money looks derisively little when compared with incomes in our modern inflated currencies. In the early nineteenth century it was a modest lower middle-class income. It may indeed have allowed a family to live in no more than 'genteel poverty', but it was certainly not a starvation wage. Genteel poverty was not the worst state to be in. It just meant the family income had to be managed carefully. It was not abject poverty or dire poverty.

Montgomery observed the reactions of the ministers and elders as Cooke read out his proposition and they each responded.

Some of them looked down in shame, others looked up in agony; but only two alternatives presented themselves to view – closed pulpits, starving children and destitute old age, or all those appalling evils avoided by uttering a solemn falsehood before God and the world.

He also felt that, apart from the timid men and those who feared for their future, there were some who would have signed anything, not having 'much faith of any kind'. He knew particularly one minister, a 'leading member of the Synod', who had freely taken the Trinitarian oath at Strabane, yet he had once heard that same man described as nothing less than an atheist. That gentleman may indeed have been an atheist. He may however have been just a person who sometimes expressed unusual or unpopular opinions and was therefore deemed to be devoid of faith. Perhaps he was a cynic who said things other people did not understand.

Cooke was of course encouraged by defeat of the Unitarians at Strabane. So were his associates in the Synod of Ulster, his aristocratic friends, and the increasing numbers in the other Protestant churches who were becoming his admirers, followers and adherents. But, as one close friend admitted, he also had enemies, in Belfast and elsewhere. Cooke himself complained that for 'upwards of two years' he had been attacked constantly in some of the newspapers and in certain other publications. He claimed he could name twenty and more editors and reporters whose attacks had been 'incessant and apparently interminable'.

He nonetheless set himself the task, during the winter of 1827/28 of consolidating what he had gained in Strabane. He was now ready to propose a system which would make it impossible for none but candidates who were sworn Trinitarians to be licensed and ordained in the Irish Presbyterian Church. And even that, as events soon made clear, was merely preliminary to cleansing the church of any Unitarians who remained, or thought they might be allowed to remain.

Cooke's proposition, which he put to the annual meeting of the Synod in Cookstown, Co Tyrone, in June 1828, was that

> every candidate for the ministry, previous to entering a theological class, should be enjoined to present himself at the annual meeting of Synod to be examined by a select committee respecting his personal religion, his knowledge of scripture, especially his views on the doctrine of the Trinity, original sin, justification by faith, and regeneration; and that no man should in future receive licence or ordination unless he professed faith in the above doctrines.

The Unitarians protested but were overruled by a majority of eighty-two. The select committee was then appointed to examine and approve or reject all candidates aspiring to be Presbyterian ministers in Ireland. The Unitarians were excluded from that committee. Fifty years later J L Porter would be pleased to record that the orthodoxy of the Presbyterian clergy was thus secured ... No Arian could thenceforth honestly enter a theological class, obtain licence, or proceed to ordination. The plan has ever since been followed by the Presbyterian Church in Ireland, and has given entire satisfaction.

The appointment of the select committee was still not all that Cooke wanted. The Unitarians were still in the church. He wanted them out altogether. He was, however, uneasy and concerned. Some of his more considerate friends, or at least those who were less vindictive, feared he might be going too far. They would have been content simply to see Unitarianism fade away in its own time as the offending ministers died or retired, one after another, and no more young Unitarians were ordained.

As it happened the Unitarians were not yet ready to accept defeat and fade away. They would try once more to nullify the propositions passed at Cookstown. In October 1828 they organised a meeting at which only Unitarians would have the right to vote, but to which the public and any ministers of religion who might be interested would be welcome as observers. Cooke did not miss the opportunity. In a letter which they published in the newspapers he and two others alleged that the meeting was to be

neither more nor less than an assembly of Arian and Socinian ministers and laymen for the purpose of counteracting the endeavours of the Synod of Ulster to restore itself to those primitive principles of Orthodoxy upon which it was originally founded.

Cooke and three other ministers arrived at the meeting accompanied, as John A Crozier later observed, by 'a large body of their adherents'. And as soon as the meeting opened Montgomery and Cooke became involved in an ill-tempered personal quarrel in which they accused each other of desecrating the Sabbath by reading the Sunday newspapers and by travelling to Dublin on public transport. Cooke thought it sinful of Montgomery to walk out and admire the natural beauty of the countryside around Coleraine on a Sunday morning instead of worshipping God in the nearest Presbyterian meeting house.

It was only when Cooke and his 'large body of adherents' withdrew that the meeting was able to complete the business for which it had been called, the publication of a statement, or remonstrance, in which the grievances of the Unitarians were again listed and their theology proclaimed. The intention was to have the remonstrance discussed at the next annual assembly of the Synod, in Lurgan the following June.

The remonstrance was never discussed in Lurgan. The appointment of John Ferrie, a Scotsman, to the chair of moral philosophy in the Belfast Academical Institute, became a more important matter. Ferrie was another Unitarian. He defeated James Carlisle of Dublin, the Synod of Ulster's own nominee for the position. And, as Professor Finlay Holmes has written in his modern biography of Cooke,

> ... it was the Ferrie appointment which dominated the 1829 synod meetings in Lurgan and the anticipated confrontation over the remonstrance never took place ... when the question of Ferrie's appointment came before the house Cooke resumed his characteristic belligerence.

The debate on the appointment of Ferrie took up so much time, and became so bitterly personal and insulting as Cooke and Montgomery assailed each other, that the Moderator who presided had to bring the proceeding to an abrupt end. The assembly then agreed to convene a special meeting at which the remonstrance and the grievances of the Unitarians would be considered. The special meeting was held in August but few ministers and fewer elders attended. Apart from William Porter, who continued to act as secretary, none of the Unitarians turned up. They had already decided at a meeting in Belfast to withdraw altogether from the Synod of Ulster. What has been known since then as the Non-Subscribing Presbyterian Church of Ireland was about to be established.

* * *

Earlier that same year Parliament had passed the Catholic Relief Act. By that enactment what is known as Catholic Emancipation had been achieved, after a long campaign of public meetings and debate in parliament led by the Catholic leader, Daniel O'Connell, and supported by the more liberal and more tolerant Protestants, among them Henry Montgomery.

Montgomery's defence of civil rights was reported in the newspapers on both sides of the Irish Sea. On one notable occasion, January 1829, he was called upon personally by William Crolly, Catholic Bishop of Down and Conor, to address an Emancipation meeting in St Patrick's R C Church in Donegall Street. That evening, as guest at a dinner in Belfast, he heard himself described by Bishop Crolly as a man who had done more for the cause of civil rights, especially when he spoke to audiences in England, than 'a whole deputation from the Catholic community could have effected'.

Most students of Irish history know the circumstances in which parliament passed the Catholic Relief Act. In June 1828 O'Connell was elected MP for Clare, but would be debarred from taking his seat in parliament if he did not swear on oath that he rejected the basic articles of the Catholic faith. O'Connell would not, of course, swear any such oath.

At that time the famous Duke of Wellington was Prime Minister. Robert Peel was Home Secretary. They both realised that something extraordinary had occurred in the Clare constituency, and could foresee many other constituencies returning Catholic MPs if O'Connell and his party put up enough candidates in the next general election. They therefore told King George the Fourth, when he hesitated to give the Royal Assent to the Catholic Relief bill, that if such elections were declared invalid there would almost certainly be another rebellion in Ireland.

The Act which Parliament passed in April 1829 declared that the 'restraints and disabilities' imposed on the Catholics of Great Britain and Ireland 'shall be from henceforth discontinued'. It therefore repealed

> ... certain Oaths and certain Declarations, commonly called the Declaration against Transubstantiation, and the Declaration against Transubstantiation and the Invocation of Saints and the Sacrifice of the Mass, as practised in the Church of Rome are or may be required to be taken, made, and subscribed by the Subjects of His Majesty, as Qualifications for sitting and voting in Parliament, and for the enjoyment of certain Offices, Franchises and Civil Rights.

But who exactly was 'emancipated' by the Catholic Relief Act? What history knows as Catholic Emancipation might have meant something to a small number of ambitious middle-class and upper-class Catholics. It meant nothing whatever to the millions of ordinary work-a-day Catholics throughout the whole of the United Kingdom, whether they were the impoverished and oppressed smallholders and labourers of rural Ireland or the emigrants living overcrowded in the slums of Britain's expanding industrial cities. None of those small farmers, labourers and industrial workers would ever have dreamed of becoming MPs or of seeking appointment to offices of state. Nor would anybody have ever considered any of them as likely candidates for such honorific employment. Not one of them had even the right to vote in municipal or parliamentary elections. Indeed, the forty-shilling freeholders, a section of the rural population that previously had the franchise, were actually deprived of their political rights by the 1829 Act. They were disfranchised, states Volume 13 of the *Oxford History of England*, in order 'to prevent O'Connell from controlling the Irish vote'.

Catholic Emancipation was therefore nothing more than the creation of opportunity for middle-class Catholics seeking office in the Protestant state. The number of people with such ambitions would have been a very small minority in the entire Catholic population.

Were Montgomery and the other emancipationists aware of all that? They may have been. More likely they were not. But even if they had been, the unexpressed rights of the impoverished millions would have meant nothing whatever to any of them. The 'democracy' they believed in was then just in its early stages. They were many more civil rights still to be fought for. Many of those rights were never even considered by democrats in the early nineteenth century.

* * *

Once the Catholic Relief Act had been passed Catholic emancipation was no longer a major political issue. For Montgomery and the other remonstrants their future as Presbyterian ministers certainly was. The Presbyterians of Ireland were by then embroiled in a sort of theological civil war, Trinitarians on the one side, Unitarians on the other. And the Unitarians had probably more support than Cooke and his colleagues expected. After two meetings, one in September and the other in October 1829, the Presbytery of Armagh, the ministers and the elders, resolved that they should

> as a body, decline the jurisdiction of the Synod [of Ulster] and retain the name and records and privileges of the Presbytery of Armagh.

That must surely have dismayed Cooke and the orthodox party. In the organisational structure of Presbyterian Churches the presbytery is a council of ministers and laymen (elders) from each of the congregations in a particular geographical area. The Presbytery of Armagh represented thirty congregations.

Cooke and the orthodox party were nonetheless determined to secure the loyalty and control of as many congregations as possible. That often meant resorting to tactics that could hardly be called gentlemanly, like sending what John Crozier called 'young probationers, with faces of brass and lungs of iron' to subject aged and ailing ministers like Samuel Arnold in Warrenpoint, to 'an almost incredible system of persecution'.

When the regular Sunday service ended at Warrenpoint the young probationers would remain in the church, despite the objections of Samuel Arnold, the elders and the congregation, and 'preach to a few discontented individuals and strangers'. That form of harassment continued, Sunday after Sunday, until after several months had passed and the magistrates dealt with the intruders.

The 'young probationers' whom Cooke sent to Warrenpoint were typical, wrote Crozier, of all the orthodox preachers who travelled to places where they assumed that the Unitarians were weak in numbers and where the ministers were aged and of a quiet and retiring disposition. They 'swarmed in all directions', preaching and praying, and terrifying vulnerable people with appalling pictures of hell and of the everlasting torment that awaited all who followed the Arian heretics.

In one man, however, they took on someone who was more than a match for all of them. He was William Glendy, the minister of Ballycarry, nephew of the Maghera man John Glendy who had escaped to America in 1798.

When Cooke and the Presbytery of Templepatrick tried to occupy the church in Ballycarry Glendy and his congregation were waiting, ready to repulse the invaders. The *Northern Whig* later reported that Cooke had driven in style from Belfast to Ballycarry in his brand new phaeton, a smart four-wheeled open carriage, and had met the Presbyters of Templepatrick, whom he had called in to help, 'in solemn and secret conclave in the village ale-house'.

He then led his friends of Templepatrick in procession towards Ballycarry Presbyterian church but was there confronted and his way blocked by a large assembly of people, reckoned to be maybe a thousand or more. His way was again blocked when he tried to enter Templecorran, the historic old churchyard where, according to folklore and legend, Presbyterianism was first preached in Ireland.

Cooke then tried to hold a meeting in the main street but had to give up. Amid the discordant cries and protests of the people he and his friends retreated back to the ale-house. The last thing he saw, as he left Ballycarry that day in his brand new phaeton, was a straw-stuffed effigy of himself ablaze in the main street.

Shortly before he was repulsed by the Unitarians of Ballycarry and his effigy burned in the main street, Cooke had been awarded an honorary doctorate of divinity by Jefferson College in the USA. And in Belfast a group of well-wishers, most of them men with money, invited him to be minister to a newly formed congregation in a splendid new church in May Street. He therefore left Killyleagh and came to May Street, and was minister there for the remainder of his life.

Meanwhile the struggle for control of churches and congregations continued, even to the extent of calling in the baronial constabulary, the magistrates and the military. That is what happened at Greyabbey in County Down in January and February 1830.

The congregations of Greyabbey, Dunmurry, Moneyrea, Ballee, and Moira, all within the Presbytery of Bangor, had seceded under the influence of their Unitarian ministers and had constituted themselves the Remonstrant Synod of Bangor. Cooke and the Orthodox could do little about either Dunmurry where Henry Montgomery was Minister, or Monyrea, where Fletcher Blakeley, a strong Unitarian, was minister. But they tried to get control of Greyabbey by asking William Montgomery, the local landowner and magistrate, to help them retain what they claimed to be

> the original right of the Orthodox members of the congregation to the use of the meeting house, which their fathers received for an Orthodox people [and] for an Orthodox minister, under the patronage of your ancestors.

Acting upon that letter and without inquiring further William Montgomery intervened. He forbade John Watson, the minister of Greyabbey, to preach in the meeting house. He put a military guard on the building and padlocked the door. Watson was arrested the following Sunday when he tried to get into the church, put under police guard and marched about, for the whole of eight or nine hours, from one magistrate to another. It was only at the end of that long, dark and fatiguing winter's day that he was set free and allowed to go home.

When Henry Montgomery wrote and explained the Unitarians' reasons for seceding from the Synod of Ulster Montgomery the magistrate realised he had been misled by Cooke and by the other five ministers who had signed the original letter. He thereupon reinstated John Watson as minister of Greyabbey, apologised, and recompensed him for the distress he had suffered.

Montgomery had by then gone to Dublin to seek government recognition for the Remonstrant Synod and to claim a share of the *Regium Donum* for the Unitarian ministers and their new church. There is no record of what transpired when he was in Dublin, apart from two or three letters written home to his wife in Dunmurry, though John Crozier was sure that he 'left a favourable impression upon the minds of the authorities'.

* * *

When those Catholics who aspired to be MPs or who sought appointment to offices of state had been accorded their rights Montgomery took up other political causes. He joined in the protest against a proposed increase in stamp duty, an important political matter in the early nineteenth century. Stamp duty was a tax on publications. It made printed information, especially the newspapers, more expensive and was therefore denounced as 'a tax on knowledge'.

In three anonymous articles in the *Northern Whig* (December 1829-January 1830) he exposed rack-renting on the County Antrim estates of the Marquis of Hertford. It was through a threatened libel suit, because of those articles, that he first met Daniel O'Connell.

In August 1830 he was the principal speaker at a public meeting which Sir Stephen May, the Sovereign (or Mayor) of Belfast, had called to enable all who were interested to consider 'the late Revolution in France as an event unparalleled in the history of the world'.

By 'the late revolution in France' Sir Stephen meant the banishment of Charles X, the last Bourbon king of France, in July 1830, and the enthronement of Louis-Phillipe, the 'Citizen King'.

Moving the address which, it was proposed, would be presented to the French Chamber of Deputies, Montgomery expressed gratification at Belfast being the first town in Ireland to declare support for the July Monarchy, adding that the revolutionary unity of the French should be 'a lesson to unhappy Ireland' whose people ought now to forget all their disputes, their differences of opinion, whether in religion or politics, and unite for the common good of their country.*

(The same sentiment would be expressed by many others long after Montgomery, by Horace Plunkett for example and the Recess Committee in 1895, and particularly by His Majesty King George the Fifth at the opening of the first parliament of Northern Ireland in 1921.)

---

*Dónal Ó Luanaigh, 'Contemporary Irish Comments Concerning the Revolution of July 1830 in France' in *Éire-Ireland*, XXII-2

At the beginning of December 1830 Montgomery was one of several liberals on the platform of the 'great reform meeting' which was held in the Belfast Court House. He was the only clergyman there and again defended his presence, as he had done at the meeting in support of the July Monarchy, by asserting that he did not lose his rights as a citizen when he became a minister of the gospel. Indeed he felt that he would be deserting his calling as a Christian if he did not, in what he considered those 'alarming times', raise his voice in defence of justice.

There were many who then believed that the reform of parliament, which is what the great reform meeting in Belfast was about, was long overdue. Democrats all over the United Kingdom had been protesting since the beginning of the nineteenth century, and even earlier, against the severe property qualifications for membership of parliament, against the undemocratically restricted franchise which gave the right to vote to no more than a very small minority of the adult male population, against the patronage and bribery that facilitated the election of MPs who were often nothing but the nominees of the landowners in whose estates the parliamentary constituencies were situated, and against a multiplicity of other corrupt practices.

Lives were lost in the early years of the campaign for reform of parliament. Eleven people were killed and 400 wounded in Manchester on 16 August 1819 when the yeomanry launched a sudden attack on a reform rally on St Peter's Fields. That tragedy is remembered in English history books as the Manchester Massacre.

In his speech to the great reform rally in Belfast, Montgomery declared that he abhorred 'all ascendancy, Catholic, Protestant, or Presbyterian'. He wished 'to see no ascendancy but that of industry, intelligence, moral right, and liberty, in short the ascendancy of the people'. The constitution of the United Kingdom should guarantee the ascendancy of the people, through an elected parliament. At least that was the principle. But what, he asked, was the practice?

Do we not all know that peers not only interfere in the choice of members of the Lower House of Parliament but that, by their simple will and influence, they return the majority of the House of Commons, thus rendering it, not what it purports to be and ought to be, a separate and independent branch of the legislature, but a subservient second chamber of the House of the Lords.

Until the appearance in politics of wealthy commoners such as Gladstone, Disraeli and the bookseller W H Smith, the aristocracy was the ruling class. Whether Whig or Tory, Liberal or Conservative they were the prime ministers and, with only rare exceptions, the cabinet ministers also. Even as late as 1861 the poet Matthew Arnold would observe that

the aristocracy still administers public affairs; and it is a great error to suppose, as many persons in England suppose, that it administers but does not govern.

In his speech to those who were seeking the reform of parliament, thirty years before Matthew Arnold made that observation, Henry Montgomery argued for the introduction of the secret ballot, in place of the simple oral declaration that voters then made in the presence of a magistrate acting as returning officer. The oral declaration, he stated

corrupts all concerned, demoralises the peasant, makes a tyrant of the landlord, puts slaves and speculators into parliament, fills the country with placemen and pensioners, places mitres on the heads of those who have no other qualifications but their political pliancy – and, worst of all, poisons the very fountain of justice by placing upon the judgement-seat, as the arbiter of men's lives and fortunes, a mere political prostitute and slave.

Montgomery assumed that the secret ballot would encourage electors to vote according to their conscience and convictions, and not as the landowner, his agent and his bailiff directed them to vote. But even so he still knew how subservient men could be, no matter what rights they had, nor what safeguards there were against corruption.

What has since been known as the Great Reform Act was passed in both houses of parliament and given the Royal Assent

in June 1832, after more than two years of political crisis and in-
stability. During those years there were urban riots which, it was
suspected, might well have been indirectly incited by certain
well-placed supporters of reform in order to intimidate the authorities. There was an organised run on the banks and insidious
threats of revolution.

The reforms granted were disappointing to those sections of
the population who expected more. A mere 217,000 new voters
were added to an electorate of 435,000 in England and Wales, yet
the total population of those two countries was then 14 million.
Most adult men and all women were still denied the right to
vote. There were separate reform acts, with the same restrictions,
for Scotland and Ireland.

* * *

Henry Montgomery's speech in support of parliamentary reform, in December 1830, was reported in several of the newspapers and thus brought to the attention of Daniel O'Connell
who had by then started a reform campaign of an entirely different sort in Ireland. O'Connell was now demanding Repeal of the
Act of Union, by which he obviously meant the restoration in
some form of the Irish Parliament that had been bribed to vote
for its own extinction in 1800. Beyond that he never explained or
even tried to explain how he thought Ireland would be governed after repeal of the Act of Union. He was nonetheless seeking to enlist others, Protestants as well as Catholics, in the
Repeal campaign.

Two weeks after the Great Reform meeting in Belfast a 'long
and plausible letter', appeared in the *Northern Whig*. It was
signed by John Lawless, a Belfast journalist who was then one of
O'Connell's must trusted colleagues. At the end of several paragraphs of unctuous praise, Lawless abjectly begged leave to
draw 'the attention of the Rev Henry Montgomery to the question of Repeal of the Union'.

A week later, O'Connell himself announced, in 'a strain of
still more emphatic eulogy', that there was never anything he
had read with greater pleasure than the speech of his 'excellent

and respected friend, the Rev Mr Montgomery' at the reform
meeting in Belfast. Never, he said, was an abler speech pro-
nounced at any public meeting. He therefore hoped that his
'friend the Rev Mr Montgomery' would now join the Repeal
campaign and help him to make Ireland the independent nation
which it ought to be.

O'Connell would not at that time have known that the previous June, when George the Fourth died, the Remonstrant Synod
had submitted to Sir Robert Peel, the Home Secretary, 'a loyal
and congratulatory address' in which they assured William the
Fourth, the newly-acclaimed king, that they were 'firmly at-
tached to the principles of the British Constitution and to His
Majesty's illustrious House', under which they had 'so long enjoyed the blessings of Civil and Religious Liberty'.

They further assured the king, and the Home Secretary, that
they would continue to impress upon their congregations, and
all other people 'with whom they were connected', a loyal and
dutiful respect for His Majesty's government, a cheerful obedi-
ence to the laws, and zealous co-operation in every measure that
may promote the peace and prosperity of the country. And they
looked with confidence to His Majesty's 'paternal care' to pro-
tect them in the exercise of those rights and privileges which
they had so far enjoyed. In his reply Sir Robert Peel informed the
Remonstrants that

> His Majesty was pleased to receive the loyal and dutiful address of
> the ministers and elders of the Remonstrant Synod of Ulster in the
> most gracious manner.

John Lawless's attempt to draw Montgomery into the Repeal
campaign induced others to reply. Several did so in letters to the
editor of the *Northern Whig*. According to John Crozier, all of
those letters were 'uncompromising in their opposition to the
schemes of O'Connell and the Repealers'. One was from 'a
member of the Reform Committee in Belfast'. Another was written by 'a Belfast Reformer'. A third was headed 'Common Sense
versus Daniel O'Connell'. And a fourth, signed 'Conscientious
Emancipationist', was presented as

an Address to the Roman Catholics of the North of Ireland on the evils of agitating at the present crisis the Repeal of the Union, and the line of conduct which it is in their interest to adopt'.

Crozier thought the letters were written by Montgomery. They may have been. They could also have been written by others, either prompted by Montgomery or independently of him. In any case the letters in the *Northern Whig* were not what annoyed O'Connell. What annoyed him was a further declaration of loyalty that a deputation of ministers and elders from the Remonstrant Synod of Ulster, the Synod of Munster, and the Presbytery of Antrim presented personally in Dublin to his excellency, the Marquis of Anglesey, Lord-Lieutenant of Ireland, in January 1831.

After stating their belief in 'the right of private judgement' and in the authority of the Bible only in matters of faith, the Remonstrants declared that

cherishing, both from hereditary descent and from personal convic-
tion, the warmest attachment to the principles of the British
Constitution, we feel it to be our duty, at the present crisis, to assure
your Excellency of our firm and faithful adherence to the connection
existing between Great Britain and Ireland. We deprecate any measure or attempt tending to relax the bonds of that connexion, being
convinced that the interests of both countries are identical, and their
prosperity inseparably conjoined.

The Remonstrants' declaration of loyalty was signed by Edward King, Moderator of the Synod of Munster, William Bruce DD, Moderator (pro tem) of the Presbytery of Antrim, and Henry Montgomery, Moderator (pro tem) of the Remonstrant Synod of Ulster. It is exactly what Ulster Unionists and Orangemen have been saying for generations, down to the present day.

In his reply, dated 20 January 1831, the Lord Lieutenant expressed his approval of the political and religious principles expressed in the declaration and added, as would any Unionist, that 'England and Ireland must stand or fall together'.

O'Connell was furious when he read in the newspapers that Montgomery, one of the influential men whom he had hoped to enlist in the Repeal campaign, had publicly reaffirmed his 'faithful adherence' to the Union of Great Britain and Ireland. On 26 January at a crowded Repeal meeting in Dublin he heaped the sort of personal insults for which he was notorious upon that 'paltry and pitiful slave', that 'fawning, cringing sycophant'. Montgomery replied, a week or so later, in a letter that was sent direct to O'Connell and to the newspapers. It filled 'several columns' in the *Dublin Evening Post*.

The letter was a long and insulting ramble, more personal than political. In it Montgomery alleged that O'Connell was a 'constitutionally arrogant and vain' man, surrounded by sycophants, living on a daily diet of flattery. And if he imagined that he personally had created the circumstances that made him important he was much mistaken.

> Had it not been for the wrongs of the Catholics of Ireland, Daniel O'Connell would, in all likelihood, never have attained to a higher rank than that of a jovial, second-rate barrister.

The letter amused Dublin Castle no end, and delighted all who wanted to see O'Connell publicly humiliated. The Lord Lieutenant wrote to tell Earl Grey, who was then Prime Minister, that

> a young Presbyterian minister in the North had done more in a single letter to defeat and crush O'Connell than all the means which the government had taken for that purpose.

Montgomery received congratulations from the ministers and laymen of the Remonstrant church, including one from John Mitchel of Newry, father of John Mitchel the Nationalist leader who was deported from Ireland in 1848. There were letters from Church of Ireland vicars, and one from a Methodist pastor in Belfast who admitted that not only did he abhor the very thought of Repeal of the Union but he never even wanted Catholics to have equal rights with Protestants.

Montgomery's letter to O'Connell was published again in the *Northern Whig* on 14 February and then printed as a pamphlet by Hodgson in Belfast. Five hundred copies were printed separately in Cork by William J Hort, one of O'Connell's former friends.

The full text of the letter can still be read as an appendix in John Crozier's first, and only, volume of the biography of Henry Montgomery.

While Montgomery, the liberal dissenter, was publicly declaring himself a constitutionalist and a friend of the government, Henry Cooke was actively demonstrating that he too believed that 'a clergyman was still a citizen and ought conscientiously to exercise all the rights of citizenship'. Furthermore, he thought it a clergyman's duty to influence the political opinions of those who were 'within the sphere of his influence'. He meant, of course, members of his own church and of his own congregation, though by then his 'sphere of influence' was extending well beyond the Presbyterian community.

Patrick Dorrian, a Catholic priest in Belfast and in later years Bishop of Down and Connor, also asserted the right of the clergy to express whatever political opinions they wanted to express. He believed, like most other Catholics, that the Act of Union should be repealed. He said so publicly. Rev Dr Ambrose Macauley has explained why Fr Dorrian took this view and why he rejected

> the admonition to the Catholic clergy, gratuitously and inconsistently given to them by both Whigs and Tories, to steer clear of politics.

The Whigs and the Tories did not offer the same advice to those parsons of the Orange persuasion whose political speeches were published regularly in all the loyalist newspapers. Fr Dorrian could therefore see no reason why a Catholic priest should not also express his political thoughts and opinions 'clearly, firmly and vigorously'.*

* * *

In 1831 Edward Stanley, Chief Secretary for Ireland, devised a system of non-sectarian elementary education in Ireland. When being taught reading, writing, arithmetic etc, Catholic children and Protestant children would be taught together. But they would receive religious instruction separately, from clergymen

---

*Ambrose Macauley, *Patrick Dorrian: Bishop of Down and Connor 1865-1885*

of their own churches, on a day of the week set apart for religious education. As Stanley put it in a letter which he wrote to
the Duke of Leinster the schools would 'admit children of all
creeds but interfere with none'. The entire system would be controlled by the Commissioners of National Education, seven men
of 'high personal character', representing the Roman Catholic
Church, the Church of Ireland, and the Presbyterian Church.

At the beginning the Catholic bishops agreed, but cautiously,
to try this new system of non-denominational, or integrated, education. Most of the Church of Ireland bishops were not sure if
they should. The Presbyterians, influenced by Henry Cooke,
were immediately hostile. Cooke even alleged that the
Commissioners were a clique of 'Radicals, Unitarians and
Roman Catholics' who had been appointed merely 'to exercise
their baleful influence against the truth'. He feared that
Protestant schoolmasters and Protestant ministers of religion
would be compelled

> not merely to permit but absolutely to encourage the teaching of
> Popery, Unitarianisn and every possible form of apostasy and infi-
> delity … and to act as the wardens of papal superstition.

The Catholics did not ask for the National schools. They were
offered, as were the Presbyterians, two places on the Board of
Commissioners. Some of the Catholic bishops were doubtful,
not, at first, because they feared any particular threat to the faith
but because the schools were forbidden to teach Irish history,
the Irish language and the literature of Ireland. John McHale, the
Archbishop of Tuam, became particularly hostile. He went further
and thought that, being by far the majority in the population of
Ireland, the Catholics should have more responsibility in the
administration of the schools, nationally and locally. This caused
division within the hierarchy but when the matter was referred
to Rome for settlement the reply was that each bishop should
decide for himself, within his own diocese, whether to accept or
reject the National schools. In the end most of the bishops accepted.

Meanwhile, as the years passed, Cooke and the Presbyterians

repeatedly objected to what the commissioners were doing or wanted to do. They rejected every compromise and accommod- ation offered. They introduced what must have seemed endless complications. Eventually the commissioners and the govern- ment gave up and let Cooke and his friends have what they wanted. What they wanted was Presbyterian schools for Presbyterian children, along, of course, with the money provided by the commissioners – taxpayer's money.

By then Edward Stanley could see that his experiment in non-sectarian education had failed. National education became national segregated education and remained so well into the twentieth century.

Unfortunately, in some places the opposition to Stanley's non-denominational schools went much further than clerical in- trigue or mere verbal obstruction. James Porter, a Presbyterian minister in Drumlee, Co Down was attacked by an armed mob when he incorporated his school in the new system and accepted the terms of the National Commissioners. Schoolhouses were, for the same reason, wrecked or burned by mobs in parts of County Tyrone. Schools had to be closed and abandoned in Antrim and Down, and in Tyrone, because of sectarian opposi- tion and threats to the schoolmasters in charge.

Yet as time would reveal, Stanley's project was more remark- able than even men of affairs could have foreseen in the 1830s. It was forty years before W E Forster's system of state elementary education in the whole of the United Kingdom. It was 150 years ahead of the state-financed integrated schools in Northern Ireland today.

* * *

The French Revolution, the publication of books such as Thomas Paine's *Rights of Man*, and the propaganda of the United Irishmen had by 1800 implanted in Ulster what the more conser- vative-minded people thought were 'exaggerated notions of popular rights'. Most Presbyterians were then democrats and liberals and some perhaps still republicans. But by the year 1830 there was an evident and 'powerful reaction' against the radicals and republicans, though more among the Presbyterian laity than on the part of the clergy. The Union of Great Britain and Ireland was by then accepted by most Presbyterians. J L Porter was certain that 'the energy, the eloquence, and the influence of Dr Cooke' was what effected that change in political outlook.

Cooke denied being either a Whig or a Tory. He said he was a Conservative and, like all Conservatives, defended the rights of property. He was also convinced that his mission, as a minister of religion with distinctive political convictions, was both to defend the Union and to 'counteract the designs of Popery'. He so influenced public opinion that through time, said Porter, Protestant Ulster became

> one of the most intensely Conservative sections of the United Kingdom.

Cooke did not, however, have the same influence on his more immediate colleagues in the Presbyterian ministry. Many were displeased when it was announced that on 30 October 1834 he would speak at a political rally on the estate of Lord Hillsborough, the High Sheriff of County Down. Porter considered the Hillsborough gathering 'one of the most influential meetings ever held in Ireland'. Lord Hillsborough was chairman. On the platform were the Marquis of Donegall, Lord Londonderry, the Earl of Clanwilliam, Lord Castlereagh, Lord Dufferin, Lord Arthur Hill, the Earl of Roden, and Henry Cooke.

One report put the audience at forty thousand, but that was certainly an exaggeration, though not so exaggerated as the figure given in the *Dublin Evening Mail* – 'not less than seventy-five thousand'. The *Northern Whig* (3 November 1834) admitted that 'the crowd was certainly very great' but that 'about ten or twelve thousand would be perhaps pretty near the truth'. Many of the people present were Orangemen from Antrim and Down or tenants who came because they had been told to attend and were afraid of offending their landlords. There were 'special constables', a sort of private police force, with white batons, white arm bands and white hats. They were there to keep order and steward the crowds.

The platform was erected across a hedge dividing two fields. One field was for the common crowd, the other was reserved for the 'gentlemen', who each paid an entrance fee of five shillings. The money collected went into the funds of the Conservative Party in Belfast.

The Church of Ireland clergy and the Tory landowners organised the Hillsborough rally to protest against the Reform Act of 1832 and the loss of what they claimed were their 'rights, safeguards and privileges'. They also feared that the Whig government, now led by Lord Melbourne, might make even more concessions to the Catholics.

And it was indeed only a few months after the Hillsborough rally, in the spring of 1835, that the government did offer O'Connell certain minor concessions in return for his support in the House of Commons and his goodwill in the wider discussion of government policy.

The clergymen who went to Hillsborough feared above all what the government might do about the tithes, one of their church's principal sources of income. The government had already appointed a commission to inquire into the status and revenues of the Church of Ireland.

The tithes had to be paid not only by members of the Church of Ireland, which was of course Protestant, but by the Catholics, the Presbyterians and whoever else was required by law to pay. The Catholics, the Presbyterians and members of the other dissenting and non-conformist churches naturally resented and often resisted that imposition. None of them had anything at all to do with the Church of Ireland. Many Ulster Presbyterians heartily disliked the Church of Ireland and often refused to pay. In 1833, for example, the arrears of unpaid tithes amounted to £1.2 million. The government made good that loss with a grant of one million pounds to the Church of Ireland.

In other parts of Ireland there had at times been armed opposition when the tithe proctors arrived, protected by soldiers and policemen, and often accompanied by bailiffs who would seize livestock in lieu of payment. Sixteen policemen, the tithe-collector, and two of the local people were killed at Hugginstown in County Tipperary, on 14 December 1831, during the worst days of what had by then become a tithe war.

Most of the Presbyterian clergy were therefore decidedly opposed to the Hillsborough rally which they regarded as nothing more than another demonstration

> of Tory politics and High Church ascendancy ... Cooke was warned against attending. He was told that if he did so he would compromise his church, and peril his position as leader of the Synod.

That is why Cooke felt that the first thing he had to do at Hillsborough was to apologise for his presence and explain that he was there not as a representative of the Presbyterian community but simply as 'a sample' of Presbyterianism – whatever that meant. He then alleged that Roman Catholics, Unitarians and infidels were united, in 'a crusade of destruction', while the Protestant churches were divided. 'That state of disunion', he declared, 'must continue no longer.' He then made an announcement that would have an enduring impact on the political history of Ulster.

> I trust I see more in this meeting than a mere eliciting of public opinion, or a mere gathering of the clans. I trust I see in it the pledge of Protestant union and co-operation. Between the divided churches I publish the banns of a sacred marriage of Christian forbearance where they differ, of Christian love where they agree, and of Christian co-operation in all matters where their common safety is concerned. I trust our union, for these holy purposes, is indissoluble, and that the God who has bound us in ties of Christian affection, and of a common faith, will never allow the recollections of the past, or the temptations of the present, to sever those whom he has thus united.

After his Hillsborough speech Cooke continued to urge the unity of all the Protestant churches as the only secure defence against those who would subvert the constitution of the United Kingdom by repeal of the Act of Union or by any other means. The more O'Connell and his followers campaigned for Repeal the more the Protestants in Ulster were determined to resist. As

Professor Finlay Holmes has observed in his biography of
Henry Cooke, the general election of 1832 was marked, for the
first time in the North of Ireland, by

> sectarianism and concern about the union between Great Britain
> and Ireland.

But that was not because the constitution was actually an
issue in the election of 1832. It was more because the
Conservative candidates in Belfast resorted to the tactic of accus-
ing their Liberal opponents of being 'doubtful on the question of
the Union'.

Casting that sort of doubt on political opponents influenced
those voters who might be undecided. It remained a tactic of the
Ulster Unionist Party well into the twentieth century, particularly
when the Northern Ireland Labour Party was winning elections
after the end of the Second World War in 1945.

Henry Cooke may not actually have inaugurated the politics
of sectarianism, though it is generally believed that he did. He
most certainly articulated, with all his powers of rhetoric and
personality, the inherent fears and feelings of a great many
Ulster Protestants, whether Conservatives or Liberals.

In reality there was no danger of the Act of Union being repealed. The reasons why have been explained quite clearly by
the historian Geróid Ó Tuathaigh in his book, *Ireland Before the
Famine 1798-1848*.

At that time nobody of any political significance or influence
in Britain would have seriously considered Repeal of the Act of
Union. Most British politicians feared what the Irish might do if
they governed their own country. They might make pacts with
England's enemies abroad, subsidise the industries and exports
of Ireland at a time when England alone was the workshop of
the world, and impose tariffs on imports from Britain. Sooner or
later Ireland might even become a foreign power.

There were of course many – the landowners, employees of
the state, clergy of the established church etc – whose material
interests were protected by the Union. But perhaps most inter-
esting of all, to quote Professor Ó Tuathaigh,

was the anti-Repeal attitude of those radicals and moderate liberals who, while acknowledging the need for reforms, refused to accept that a national legislature was a prerequisite for better government in Ireland.

Among the anti-Repeal radicals and the moderate liberals were, of course, those Remonstrant Presbyterians who had assured the Lord Lieutenant that they were loyal to the Crown and the constitution, including Henry Montgomery himself when he contemptuously rejected the flattering overtures of O'Connell and John Lawless.

* * *

Through time Henry Cooke felt that Ulster was his province. He resented anyone who came to express opinions or promote policies with which he disagreed. He considered such people 'invaders'. Indeed that was how he described John Smethurst, the Unitarian, in 1821. And it was how he regarded John Ritchie, a Scottish clergyman, who came to Belfast in March 1836.

Ritchie was the leader of a movement known as Voluntaryism. The Voluntarists were Presbyterian ministers and laymen who believed that neither their own church nor any of the other churches should accept government grants, subsidies or endowments. In their view churches in the United Kingdom should be independent, as they were in the USA.

In those days the Church of Ireland was the church of a distinct Protestant minority, in conspicuous association with the landowning class, wealthy, established and state-endowed. Its income seemed safe and assured. It was the church of the Orange Order.

The Presbyterian churches in Ireland, and in Britain, received their endowment in the form of the *Regium Donum*.

Maynooth College in Kildare, where young Irishmen studied to be Catholic priests, had been state-endowed since 1795. The Catholic priests would have had their equivalent of the *Regium Donum* early in the nineteenth century if the bishops had not rejected the government's terms and conditions.

The main churches were therefore all getting money from the

government. The Voluntarists alleged that by accepting government money the churches forfeited much of what should have
been their Christian freedom. A committee representing the
Voluntarists in Belfast arranged Dr Ritchie's visit and announced that on 15 March he would speak at a social evening in
the Music Hall in May Street.

As there were then only few Voluntarists in Belfast, most
public men would simply have left them to have their social
evening and let them hear what Ritchie had to say – but not
Henry Cooke. He intervened. He told the Voluntarists he would
be at the meeting. And he was there, along with more of 'his
friends and adherents' than the organisers of the evening expected and certainly more than were welcome.

When Ritchie had finished speaking Cooke stood up, amidst
'a storm of cheers' from those who were quite obviously his
friends, and hisses from others who were clearly not. He insisted
on being heard, despite the objections of the chairman. To him
Ritchie was an invader whose 'very presence in Belfast was a
challenge'. Ritchie's 'speech that evening was a challenge'. Now
he, Henry Cooke, was there to accept the challenge and meet
Ritchie 'in fair and open controversy' at a suitable time and
venue.

When Cooke and Ritchie met again, on the evening of 17
March, the Music Hall was packed, because in those days, just as
today, religion and politics combined could bring a great many
people in a place like Belfast 'to a state of frenzy', especially if
they were all together in one hall.

Cooke arrived on time even though he had been ill that
morning and had difficulty making his way to the Music Hall.
He heard the chairman, Dr R J Tennent, open the meeting with
the observation that

> no man should be called upon to pay for the religious instruction of
> another, against the light of his own conscience.

Cooke would seize upon that observation when, during his
contribution to the debate, he launched a sectarian attack on
Maynooth College and on the schools in which Catholic nuns

and Catholic priests taught Catholic children. As he spoke it became evident that, in his view, there was nothing whatever
wrong in the government being generous with taxpayers'
money so long as the money went to the Presbyterians and the
established Protestant churchmen, but that it was outrageous
that anything at all should be given to the Roman Catholics. And
that, he said, was the sincerely-held opinion of many 'hundreds
and thousands' of Ulster Protestants. He spoke about

> Maynooth [to which] some nine thousand a year is annually voted
> by the British Parliament for the exclusive education of Roman
> Catholic priests, [and about] a Popish school, held within the very
> precincts of a nunnery, a monastery, or a chapel, with nuns, monks,
> and lay brothers as teachers, with Doyle's Catechism for a school-
> book, teaching small stealing or small lying to be venial sins, and
> angel-worship, or staff-worship, to be holy and righteous services.

Nor did Dr Ritchie himself miss the chance, when he spoke,
to express his own little bit of sectarian bias. He declared that, in
his view, the *Regium Donum* 'degraded the Synod of Ulster to the
level of Maynooth'. The Voluntarists hoped they could 'rescue
the Synod of Ulster from the system of *Regium Donum*' princi-
pally because it was the late Lord Castlereagh who had determined how the money would be distributed. Castlereagh, said
Ritchie, was

> a man of whom it has been justly said that the best action of his life
> was that by which it was ended.

Ritchie obviously knew that from as early as 1803, when he
was Chief Secretary for Ireland, Castlereagh had sought to control and direct the Presbyterian clergy through distribution of
the *Regium Donum*. In this he had the willing and no doubt ener-
getic assistance of Alexander Knox, his private secretary, along
with Robert Black in Derry, and even William Bruce, headmaster of the Belfast Academy. Professor Finlay Holmes has explained, in his biography of Henry Cooke, how Castlereagh,
Knox, Robert Black and Bruce set up their scheme.

First of all, as Ritchie said, the total amount of the *Regium
Donum* was considerably increased. Then, instead of being given

as a block grant to the Synod of Ulster the money was paid individually to each minister through a government-appointed
agent, known as the Almoner of the *Regium Donum*. The almoner, himself a Presbyterian minister, would receive an appropriate and quite generous salary for managing the fund, as well
as his own share of the *Regium Donum*. Finally, to qualify for the
Regium Donum each minister had to swear an oath of loyalty to
the Crown in the presence of two magistrates.

Castlereagh and his associates were certain that the revised
and redistributed *Reguim Donum* would transform the Presbyterian ministers into 'a subordinate aristocracy' upon whom the
government could rely. Robert Black thought that the better
salaries they were receiving would enable the younger clergy to
marry into 'families of repute and influence'.

It might be assumed because of their political association
with Lord Castlereagh that Robert Black and William Bruce
were orthodox Presbyterians, like Henry Cooke. They most certainly were not. Like Montgomery and the other Remonstrants
they were of the Arian, Unitarian, or 'New Light' persuasion.
Their theology and their politics together refuted the belief that
politically the Orthodox were all loyal and all the Unitarians dis-
loyal. John Glendy of Maghera was not a Unitarian, neither was
Sinclair Kelburn of Belfast. They were, nonetheless, both United
Irishmen. Kelburn's portrait, pierced by the sword of a militia
officer who came too late to make an arrest, remained on proud
display in Rosemary Street Presbyterian Church for more than
150 years after the rebellion.

Another misapprehension is that most Ulster Presbyterians
were republicans in '98. It is true that many were. Nonetheless, it
is also true that at least twice between 1791 and the outbreak of
the rebellion the Synod of Ulster assured the Viceroy, in addresses sent directly to Dublin, that the majority of Presbyterians
were peaceful, law-abiding and loyal. When the synod met in
August 1798, belatedly because of the rebellion in June, all present

without division ... adopted humbly-worded addresses to the King

and the Lord Lieutenant [and lamented] with the deepest humilia-
tion the conduct of a few unworthy members.

Those 'few unworthy members' were the laymen and ministers who had fought in the rebellion and were by then under
sentence of death, in prison, or compelled to leave Ireland and
live in the USA.

The synod next voted a donation of £500 to HM Treasury, the
church's contribution towards the 'defence of the kingdom', and
ordered all the presbyteries

> under pain of severe censure to inquire into the political activities of
> ministers, elders and probationers.

Lord Castlereagh committed suicide on the morning of 12
August 1822. That was what Ritchie meant when he referred to
the way in which his life had ended. In life and in death he was
hated everywhere. In 1819 the poet Shelley wrote:

> I met Murder on the way.
> He wore a mask like Castlereagh.

The debate between Ritchie and Cooke continued all through
that night in March 1836, until at dawn the next day the audience and the speakers decided it was time to go home. But that
was just an adjournment. They came back in the evening to continue the debate. This time admission was by ticket only. That
made Cooke suspect that the Voluntarists had taken advantage
of the adjournment to distribute more tickets to their own supporters than they had allocated to his friends. He thus accused
them of having packed the meeting when, as the first speaker
this time, he opened the proceedings.

After that he tried to defend the memory of Lord
Castlereagh, who he feared had become the victim of 'perennial
hate'. Castlereagh was 'a great man whose slumbering ashes had
been disturbed' by the Voluntarists. He continued his defence of
Castlereagh but in language that became increasingly obscure
and elaborate.

> Charity! Charity! where is that mantle with which thou hast been
> wont to cover the multitude of a neighbour's transgressions? Is it

now the office of the loudest advocate to tear the mantle aside, and
expose to the rudest gaze the errors of both the living and the dead –
the errors of a mind exhausted with the toils of thought – the error
of the frenzied hour when reason reels and lunacy is in the ascen-
dant? Oh! might not the act of that unhappy hour be consigned to
the recesses of oblivion, or charitably be supposed to lie beyond the
verge of accountability.

Such oratory would be considered quite extraordinary today,
yet it must have impressed the citizens of Belfast in the spring of
1836. An American clergyman called Blackwood, a friend of
Cooke's, had a seat in front of the platform. From there he could
observe the audience's reaction. He afterwards recorded that as
Cooke

concentrated his colossal sentences, as his voice rose in majesty
through the hall, it was a striking scene to witness the spellbound lis-
teners leaning forward, breathless, electrified, and at length, when
the sense was complete, as if the soul was satisfied, falling back in a
mass to rest. It was as if the wand in the hand of a mighty magician
had been swaying the audience to and fro according to his will.

Cooke spoke for five hours. He admitted, during that
marathon tirade, that by accepting his share of the *Regium
Donum* he was in the pay of the state but denied he had thereby
forfeited his independence. He claimed that whoever took the
trouble to search, as he had searched, would find amply justific-
ation for the endowment of churches in the Bible, both in the
Hebrew chronicles and in the Christian gospels. He insulted,
with sarcasm and innuendo, anyone who interrupted, or even
tried to make a passing comment.

Ritchie's reply to Cooke continued for another three hours. It
must therefore have been the middle of the night before anyone
else got an opportunity to say anything. The debate continued
until six o'clock the next morning. That was when the speakers
and the audience finally decided it was time to go home. The
debate on Voluntaryism was over, with Cooke and his party
claiming that 'Voluntaryism had received a blow from which it
would never recover'.

That was most certainly an unfounded exaggeration.

Through time, in fact during the lifetime of Henry Cooke himself, the English Presbyterians would forego their *Regium Donum* and become both Unitarian and independent, the Church of Ireland would be disestablished and left to raise its own income, the annual parliamentary grant to Maynooth College would be stopped, and the Presbyterians in Ireland would get no more state money, no more *Regium Donum*, neither for the Orthodox nor for the Remonstrants.

* * *

When William the Fourth died in June 1837 the Tories and the Orangemen thought they could have the Duke of Cumberland made king. The duke was an Orangeman, or at least suspected of being in one of the English lodges. He was, however, sent to Hanover, the land from which his ancestors had come to England early in the eighteenth century. Princess Victoria, the choice of the Whigs, succeeded to the Throne. The Orangemen and the Tories then really did fear that, with Lord Melbourne still Prime Minister, the Roman Catholics would demand more and be conceded more. Henry Cooke had the same fear.

On Sunday 20 August he preached a sermon to which he gave the title 'Signs of the Times', and in which he again declared it was the duty of Christian clergymen to advise and guide their people, politically as well as in matters of faith and morals. He was convinced that it was the courage of Martin Luther and Philip Melanchthon, not the chivalry of the German nobility or the hardihood of the peasantry, that had liberated Saxony from 'the iron fangs of the Pope', that the 'learning of Melville and the thunder of Knox' had freed Scotland, and that the Puritan fathers had established 'the imperishable liberties' of England. The text upon which he preached was God's message to the prophet Ezekiel:

> I have made thee a watchman unto the house of Israel: therefore hear the word of my mouth and give them warning from me.

Upon that text he warned his congregations to:

> Take heed! Beware of Rome ecclesiastical ... beware of Rome politi-

cal which enforceth a yoke, as Herod. And whether these things be introduced under a Protestant name and disguise or whether in their own proper Roman garb and name, describe with equal truth, warn with equal faithfulness, and denounce them with equal authority.

J L Porter observed that the state of public affairs at that time, and especially the 'noisy agitations' of O'Connell and the Catholics, made Cooke the more determined to consolidate the union of all Protestants. Earlier in the summer of 1837 the Synod of Ulster had resolved, on a motion put by Cooke, that it was 'the bounden duty' of all Protestants to unite in defence of 'the glorious principles of civil and religious liberty' which were then threatened by what was alleged to be the co-ordinated assaults of 'Popery and Infidelity.' He implemented that resolution by inviting 'the leading clergy and gentry' to attend a meeting in May Street church on Thursday 31 August and there consider the formation of a Protestant Defence Association. The people who attended that meeting assembled 'long before the hour appointed'. When the meeting began every seat in the church was occupied.

Hugh McNeile, an English parson, renowned and veteran defender of the Protestant cause, was one of the speakers. He claimed that Henry Cooke was as well-qualified as Martin Luther, John Calvin, Thomas Cranmer or John Knox for the particular work God had chosen him to do.

On 19 October Cooke appeared again in the company of the 'leading nobility and gentry', this time at a political banquet in Belfast. There the theme of his hour-long speech was, once more, the 'difficulties and dangers that threatened Protestantism'. He now claimed that it was from Protestantism alone that the constitution of the United Kingdom derived 'its power of perpetual renovation'. Furthermore, the future of the United Kingdom depended entirely upon Ulster. He again warned that

> were any circumstances to subvert the Presbyterianism of Ulster the union of the three kingdoms would not be worth a twelvemonth's purchase.

In January 1841, Cooke thought he had been given what must have been his long-desired opportunity directly to confront the papist enemy.

At the end of the parliamentary session in August 1840 Daniel O'Connell announced that he would spend the recess campaigning for Repeal of the Union at meetings all over Ireland, or at least in those parts of Ireland where he knew he would be welcome. The friends of Repeal in Belfast thereupon decided they should be included. They therefore invited O'Connell to dine with them in Belfast and address a public meeting afterwards. Belfast, they assured him, was one of the places where he would be welcome. At first O'Connell was not sure and it was only after seeking the advice of friends and taking time to consider the invitation that he decided to accept. The earliest date he had free was the middle of January 1841.

On 5 January Cooke sent O'Connell a letter in which he suggested that the proposed Repeal meeting in Belfast, instead of being a 'one-sided harangue', should be an equally-divided discussion between Cooke himself and O'Connell. Everything would be arranged by a committee composed of an equal number of Repealers and anti-Repealers. Each side would receive exactly the same number of entrance tickets, for which there would be no charge. The subject to be discussed would be

> The advantages or disadvantages of Repeal of the Union to Ireland – in its bearing on agriculture, manufactures, general trade, safety of the present settlement of all property, and the protection of civil and religious liberty.

If Cooke had ended his letter with that proposition he might have received a written reply, either accepting or politely declining the challenge. But that is what he did not do. He added another two or three paragraphs of insult and recrimination which infuriated O'Connell and left him in no mood to send Cooke even a formal acknowledgement. His reply took the form of a speech to the Repeal Association in Dublin. There he made fun of Cooke, called him daddy Cooke, the cock o' the North, the boxing buffoon, and names like that. And he firmly rejected the challenge to debate Repeal of the Union saying if he accepted it would look as though he were taking on the whole Presbyterian community, and the Presbyterians, as everybody knew, were not all bigots like Henry Cooke. O'Connell went on to state that whenever he did visit Belfast it would be in style, with local processions and rallies as he passed through Drogheda, Dundalk, Newry and even Lisburn, a town which is only seven miles from Belfast.

When the processions and rallies were announced and when particularly the town of Lisburn was mentioned the authorities in Dublin were understandably concerned. They feared that O'Connell's processions, especially any held on the near approaches to Belfast, could be dangerously unsettling. A 'considerable force' of the Enniskillen Dragoons was therefore ordered to march immediately from Dundalk to Belfast. A 'large body of artillery', a battery of four guns, and 800 men of the 99th Regiment were dispatched from Charlemont Fort in County Armagh. Extra policemen arrived, under the command of Captain Flinter, with instructions 'to aid the local Constabulary, if necessary, in the preservation of the public peace'.

O'Connell wisely cancelled the processions. When he did travel to Belfast, on Saturday 16 January 1841, it was in his own private coach with three of his closest friends. He arrived at six o'clock on that dark winter's evening and went straight to his rooms in the nearby Royal Hotel. On Sunday morning he did not walk to Mass, which is what many people expected, no doubt hoping they would see the Liberator in person as he passed along Hercules Street to St Patrick's Church in Donegall Street. He and his friends stayed in the hotel that day and heard Mass privately. On Sunday evening he attended a reception in the offices of *The Vindicator*, the local Catholic newspaper.

O'Connell stayed indoors on Monday, met a deputation of local traders, and at four in the afternoon appeared on the balcony of the Royal Hotel to ask a crowd who had gathered to disperse and go home. He had no public engagements until seven that evening. He would then attend a dinner in the Pavilon, an old theatre in Chichester Street, where Robert McDowell, a 'Liberal Protestant' would preside.

According to *The Repealer Repulsed*, which was published afterwards as 'a correct narrative of the rise and progress of the Repeal invasion of Ulster', there were not more than six or seven other Liberal Protestants at the dinner. Furthermore, McDowell was the only Protestant 'who could be prevailed upon' to act as chairman. Most of the audience were Catholics, among them two bishops and several of the local priests.

O'Connell was markedly conciliatory that evening. First of all he apologised for anything harsh he might have said about the people of Belfast, claimed he would do as much for an Orangeman as he would for a Catholic, mentioned Orangemen in Dublin whom he had helped personally when they were in difficulties, and declared himself an advocate of civil and religious liberty all over the world, not just in Ireland or the British Isles.

And so Monday night 'passed tranquilly', though the author of *The Repealer Repulsed* attributed that tranquillity not to the tone of O'Connell's speech but to 'the admirable disposition' of the policemen and the soldiers. On Tuesday

> strangers, from all parts of the country, poured into town, influenced, for the most part, by curiosity to hear Mr O'Connell's far-famed oratory ... at an early hour in the forenoon, the neighbourhood of the Pavilion was literally besieged by crowds anxious to obtain admission.

O'Connell had been billed to speak to a public meeting in the Pavilion at 11 o'clock on Tuesday morning but he changed the venue when he saw that the Pavilion could not accommodate all the people who had come to hear him. He may also have been told that Cooke would be there, along with his cheer-leaders and a gang of hecklers. He therefore sent word that instead of speaking in the Pavilion he would address an open-air meeting from the balcony of the Royal Hotel. The Pavilion was thereupon deserted, and the crowd, estimated at 5,000, gathered outside the hotel. Of that crowd many were people who had just come to see and hear O'Connell, though at least one-third, it was estimated, were committed Repealers. There was in addition a band of 'sturdy anti-Repealers who spared not their voices on the occasion'.

O'Connell began by recalling the democratic traditions of the town of Belfast, back into the eighteenth century, before the parliament of Ireland was obliterated by the Act of Union. He then defied any man to call the Union anything but 'an imposition practised upon the brave people of Ireland by force and fraud', secured by gifts of titles and sinecures, and the distribution of £3 million in bribes. He was confident that there were now good financial reasons for Repeal. Ireland's share of the National Debt had increased enormously since the Union. Taxes had also increased. The drain of money out of the country, particularly in the form of rents paid to absentee landowners, had increased fourfold.

He reminded his friends, as he closed his speech, that they should remain always on the right side of the law. Whoever violated the law, whatever the political objective, merely strengthened the enemies of Ireland.

While O'Connell was speaking the 'sturdy anti-Repealers' in the audience were doing their best to wreck the meeting. They kept up a constant barrage of hooting, hissing, ironical applause and loud laughter in order to drown O'Connell's voice. But all their activities proved, said O'Connell, was that the case he was making for Repeal of the Act of Union was more than they could contend with.

That evening he attended a social reception in the Music Hall but left early because, as the author of *The Repealer Repulsed* observed, a stone-throwing mob had gathered and had already broken several of the windows.

> ... One stone was thrown with such force as to cut right through the blind inside [and] dash to pieces several lamps of the splendid chandelier suspended from the ceiling.

Some of that mob followed O'Connell back to the Royal Hotel. They gathered outside and hurled stones into the room in which he was sitting with his friends. By then the streets around that part of the town were packed with people, some the supporters of O'Connell and some his sworn enemies. As soon as the police dealt with an unruly mob in one place violence broke out somewhere else. They had to place a guard of armed constables on the Royal Hotel for the remainder of the night.

O'Connel left Belfast on Wednesday morning and travelled to Donaghadee, via Newtownards, under police escort all the way. From Donaghadee he sailed to Portpatrick, and from there travelled on to attend meetings and fulfil other engagements in England and Scotland. He felt, as he sailed away, that his visit to Belfast had been worth while and that there were plenty of people there who really supported Repeal of the Act of Union.

Cooke and his friends would now prove that O'Connell was mistaken and that in Belfast and throughout all Ulster there was far more opposition to Repeal than support. The following notice had already appeared in the local newspapers:

> The undersigned request a Meeting of the Nobility, Clergy, Gentry and other friends of the British Constitution and Connexion, in Antrim, Down and the contiguous Northern Counties to be held in Belfast, upon Thursday, the 21st January 1841, at Eleven o'clock, A.M. for the purpose of expressing their opinion in opposition to the attempt, now for the first time undisguisedly made in Ulster, to effect Repeal of the Union.

The undersigned were themselves 'the principal Nobility, Gentry and Clergy of the Province of Ulster', all of them Tories and probably all convinced, to quote Simon Armstrong, the High Sheriff of Fermanagh, that no one could be a Protestant, asserting his right to read the Bible, and at the same time 'not be a Conservative and a loyal man'. All who were not Bible-reading Protestant Conservatives were, according to High Sheriff Armstrong, 'enemies to the country'.

What was published in *The Repealer Repulsed* as 'A Full and Authentic Report of the Two Grand Conservative Demonstrations', in Belfast on 21 and 22 January 1841, listed the sponsors of those events as:

41 Peers and Noblemen

14 Right Honourables and Honourables

18 Baronets

32 Members of Parliament

11 High Sheriffs

6 Lord Lieutenants of counties

98 Deputy Lieutenants

335 Magistrates

271 Clergymen of the Established Church

28 Methodist Ministers

28 Barristers.

It is obvious, from that long list of honourables, right-honourables, etc, that the 'two great Conservative demonstrations' must have been planned weeks earlier, probably as soon as it was certain O'Connell would be coming to Belfast.

The 'great demonstrations' began with several minor speakers, all of whom must have been insufferably dull, judging from 'the full and authentic report'. Cooke was the main attraction. It was he whom everyone had come to hear. But if what he had to say was his case against Repeal of the Act of Union O'Connell had every good reason for rejecting his challenge to debate the matter.

Much of Cooke's speech was an attempt to portray O'Connell as a liar and a political trickster. Much more of it was the allegation that the Protestants in Ireland had been repeatedly and cruelly persecuted – during the reign of 'Bloody Mary', when the 'Old English' and the 'Old Irish' Catholics rebelled in 1641, and when, in 1689, James the Second signed the enactments of 'his mock parliament in Dublin'.

Cooke then added a fourth to what he termed 'O'Connell's three periods of Popish ascendancy'. This time the persecuted Protestants were 'the unhappy men and women who fell victim at Scullabogue barn and Wexford Bridge' in 1798.

The audience of Conservative ladies and gentlemen must have been deeply moved by Cooke's portrayal of those awful persecutions. But they also enjoyed his sarcastic style of oratory and his mordant sense of humour. They laughed and applauded where they were expected to laugh and applaud, cheered often, and concurred with enthusiastic hear-hears.

There was much loud and prolonged laughter when Cooke made fun of the Pavilion as a place that was once a menagerie with wild animals on show. There 'the great O'Connell' and his friends had gathered to promote Repeal of the Union.

He obviously forgot that he himself was at that moment speaking in a temporary structure that was used often as a circus, a building in Wellington Place where clowns tripped and tumbled, and animals performed tricks for the amusement of little children, and for adults with the mentality of children.

T H Witherow was studying for the Presbyterian ministry when he attended that great Conservative demonstration. Many years afterwards when he himself was a professor of theology he recalled that

> when perused in the study the style of the speech was not perhaps as pure and elevated as a great effort in oratory ought to be. But it had one quality – it was effective. It sprung from the occasion, and gave fine expression to the feelings of the time.

In other words, Cooke articulated the prejudices of the noble mob who were his audience. His speech was the sort of propaganda they wanted to hear. And that, in the simplest terms, was that neither he nor they, nor any member of the Protestant Ascendancy, would ever submit to government by the Catholic majority in Ireland.

Some historians have been impressed by that part of the speech – at the very end – in which Cooke attributed the nineteenth century economic expansion of Belfast entirely to the Union and to what he called 'the genii of Protestantism and liberty'. His argument was that before the Union Belfast was nothing more than a village, 'studded with thatched cottages'. Now, forty years after the Union, there were factories, warehouses, and a wide harbour crowded with ships.

> Our merchants are welcomed in every land, and the energies of their industry, and the profits of their toils, are only surpassed by their honourable character – (loud and vehement cheers) – the basis

of their prosperity, and the character of its continuance. (Continued cheering). In one word more I have done with my argument – Look at Belfast and be a Repealer – if you can.

Cooke's economic argument in defence of the Union seems rational, and indeed is rational, but only up to a point. Otherwise it is specious and misleading. It implies that had there not been an Act of Union Belfast would have remained a village studded with thatched cottages. That in turn implies that the parliament of Ireland, which was entirely and exclusively Protestant during the whole of the eighteenth century, was devoid of that 'genii of Protestantism and liberty' to which Cooke attributed economic success. Furthermore, neither Protestant economics nor the Act of Union can explain the presence of some very successful Catholic businessmen in Dublin, Cork and elsewhere before the Union, and in Belfast afterwards.

But even apart from the 'genius' of Protestant economics, the linen industry and the cotton industry went back in Belfast and elsewhere in the North long before the Act of Union. Belfast was manufacturing glass, chemicals, soap and muslin cloth, and refining sugar – to mention just a few products – when it was, according to Cooke, nothing more than a village of thatched cottages. William Ritchie came from Greenock in 1793 to build two new graving docks and start a shipbuilding industry. Ships were needed. Belfast was about to become a town of ship-owners. Indeed the *Hibernia*, the first ship that Ritchie built in Belfast, was built for Henry Joy McCracken, or at least for the business in which McCracken's family was engaged. Theobald Wolfe Tone actually saw McCracken's ship soon after it was launched. He mentioned it in his autobiography.

Trade and industry were expanding in Belfast before the Act of Union. It would be irrational to assume that those trades and industries would not have continued to expand had there not been an Act of Union.

After his speech at the great Conservative demonstration Cooke was acclaimed by his friends and admirers in press and pulpit as the invincible defender of the Union, but, it was feared, he might now be in danger. It was therefore decided that he be presented with a testimonial in a form which would 'secure a provision for his family should his life fall a sacrifice to his patriotism'. A committee was formed and an appeal published. Eventually

> the sum of two thousand pounds [was] raised and presented to the family of Dr Cooke ... a graceful and appropriate acknowledgement of eminent and successful services.

Cooke did not meet O'Connell face to face. Montgomery apparently did, some months after the Liberator's departure from Belfast. John Crozier later referred, in a pamphlet which was published by the Ulster Unitarian Christian Association in May 1888, to Montgomery's

> notable encounter with Daniel O'Connell in the Theatre Royal, Dublin, in 1841, and the second check there given by him to the 'Liberator', in the zenith of his power, and surrounded by his lieges, in the very citadel of his strength.

* * *

Cooke and Montgomery had one other matter to settle before they parted company and went their separate ways in the years that remained to them. Who owned the churches, meeting houses and dwellings that the Remonstrant clergy and congregations continued to occupy and use after they left the Synod of Ulster in 1829? Cooke and the Synod, known since 1840 as the General Assembly of the Presbyterian Church, claimed ownership on the grounds that those properties belonged to congregations that were originally Orthodox, not Unitarian. They felt their claim was legally vindicated when, in 1842, the Law Lords declared, in the particular case of Lady Hewley's Charity, that 'the intention of the founder of any religious or charitable trust must be construed as only meant to benefit those whose opinions were legal at the time of the foundation'.

That judgement was bound to effect the Unitarians who did not have any legal status in England until 1813 and in Ireland not until 1817. Thus, wrote John Crozier,

> virtually the entire religious properties of the English Unitarians

and of the Irish Non-Subscribing Presbyterians were at the mercy of any professing Trinitarians who might wish to appropriate them.

The Unitarians in England appointed a 'large and influential defence committee' to promote their claims, though it was soon evident that they could rely on somebody immeasurably more powerful than a committee. Sir Robert Peel, the Prime Minister, was markedly sympathetic to their cause, it being said that some of his own family and relatives were Unitarians. But whatever the support the Unitarians could expect or the legal claims of their opponents, the matter could be settled only by an Act of Parliament.

But would the Unitarians in Ireland be included? That is what took Montgomery to London in June 1843. Cooke was also there, along with his long-time friend and colleague, Robert Stewart, the Presbyterian minister of Broughshane. Stewart was an intellectual and a staunch Trinitarian. He and Cooke wanted to bankrupt the Unitarians, materially as well as ideologically. They failed. Cooke probably did not even then realise how much he was personally disliked in certain circles of government. Sir James Graham, the Home Secretary, for example, thought him a violent headstrong man.*

Montgomery, on the other hand was well received in London and his case for the Remonstrants considered sympathetically. The protection of the Dissenters' Chapels Act, which was passed in 1844, was extended to the ecclesiastical property of the Unitarians in Ireland. That was another defeat for Henry Cooke.

It came at a time when many of his colleagues and former friends among the Orthodox were beginning to see that he was indeed overbearing and overfond of power. He suffered another defeat in 1845 when he was not appointed president of Queen's College, Belfast, a constituent college of the government's new, non-sectarian university in Ireland, though on that occasion he was recompensed by being appointed agent, with a salary of £400 a year, for distribution of the *Regium Donum* to the orthodox Presbyterians.

---

*R Finlay Holmes, *Henry Cooke*

Cooke is almost always portrayed as the anti-Catholic original whose prejudices influenced both the weaker-willed of his
Protestant contemporaries in Ireland and the generations since.
But while that might be true in a certain sense, it would not be
entirely true. Cooke was not alone. There was much more highly-
organised anti-Catholicism in Britain during Cooke's lifetime
than there was in the Protestant province of Ulster.

In *Anti-Catholicism in Victorian England* (which was awarded
the Thirwall Prize in 1967), E R Norman refers to the circulation
of 'a huge volume of no-popery literature' in Britain. He found
that 'crude engravings' depicting the massacre of the French
Protestants (the Huguenots) on St Bartholomew's Day in 1572
were 'almost as familiar to the Victorians as the Bible itself' and
that the rites, liturgy and doctrines of the Roman Catholics

> seemed to some Protestants mildly derisive, to others downright
> wicked, and to some, even perverted.

Such were the views of Catholicism held not only by the un-
sophisticated British public but also by many members of parliament, clergy of the Church of England and parsons in the independent churches. In his introduction to a nineteenth century
edition of Foxe's *Book of the Martyrs*, Ingram Cobbin, a Protestant
clergyman, described Roman Catholicism as 'an inhuman system'. He said that parents should teach their children and they
in turn their children 'to dread and oppose' Roman Catholicism.

Foxe's *Book of the Martyrs*, first published in 1563, was one of
the earliest books of the English Reformation. E R Norman
thought it 'probably the best-known text in the very ample library of British anti-Catholic literature'.

There were lobby divisions and long debates in parliament
when, in 1845, the government considered increasing the grant
which was paid annually to Maynooth College, the Catholic
seminary in Ireland. Outside parliament there were angry anti-
Maynooth demonstrations the length and breadth of the country. Cooke's friend Hugh McNeile led protest demonstrations in
Liverpool.

People who gathered for a public meeting in Covent Garden were told that the Catholic Church was 'the great enemy' and the 'foe of domestic virtue'. They heard Rome accused of murdering even those heretics who recanted and begged forgiveness.

Up and down the country [E R Norman has written] this sort of stuff stirred the muddy religiosity of the excited meetings. Churchmen acquitted themselves no better than dissenters. Audience participation was warm.

The intellectual writer Harriet Martineau thought the whole of English society had gone mad.

In such circumstances Cooke was in much demand as a speaker and was invited often to Exeter Hall, the national venue of anti-Catholicism in Britain. He received letters of support and encouragement from all parts of the kingdom. Speaking in parliament, the Prime Minister once compared him to Henry Phillpotts, the Bishop of Exeter, an ageing defender of the Protestant constitution. A man by name of McCrie, writing from Edinburgh, invited him to assume leadership of the national campaign against the Catholics. Cooke declined that flattering request, saying that he would have quite enough to do defending 'the truth' in Ulster and supporting the sparse and scattered Presbyterian congregations in the south and west of Ireland.

Meanwhile those were the years when the annual crop of potatoes, the only food for millions of Irish farmers and their families, was lying black and putrid in the soil. Men, women and children were dying of starvation and disease, not just in hundreds or in thousands but in hundreds of thousands. Many more died on the 'coffin ships' that carried those fleeing from the famine across the Atlantic to Canada and the USA. The workhouses all over Ireland were overcrowded with the sick and the dying. Yet, as Finlay Holmes states in his biography of Henry Cooke,

there is strangely little in the records of the General Assembly [about] the bitter experience of the years of famine.

On the evening of Tuesday 4 December 1850 'the rank and

wealth' of Belfast, and of most places within reach of the town, assembled in May Street Church to hear Cooke deliver a lecture on 'The Present Aspect and Future Prospects of Popery'. The church was crowded. The Mayor of Belfast presided. Cooke spoke for three-and-a-half hours. J L Porter later recalled that at that time 'the subtle advances of Popery began again to be felt and feared in England' and that Henry Cooke was 'among the first to observe the danger and sound the alarm'. Cooke may indeed have been among the first to sound the alarm, or he may have been responding to a wider anti-Catholic movement that was by then already well organised.

In September 1850 the Pope issued a rescript in which he named twelve senior Catholic priests to be bishops in England. He appointed Nicholas Wiseman, now a cardinal, Archbishop of Westminster. Wiseman was returning happily from Rome when, during a stop at Vienna, he read in *The Times* what sort of reception was awaiting him in London. What he read was a denunciation of the new Catholic hierarchy.

The Pope, said *The Times*, had mistaken the traditional tolerance of the English people for indifference. The arbitrary appointment of the twelve bishops had exposed 'the power which Rome would exercise if she could'. Furthermore, the assumption of bishoprics and territorial ecclesiastical titles, by anybody other than the clergy of the established Protestant churches in England and in Ireland, had been made illegal by the Catholic Relief Act of 1829.

That part of the 1829 Act could, in effect, apply only to Great Britain, not to the whole of the United Kingdom. In Ireland there already were two hierarchies, one Catholic and the other Protestant. The Irish bishops and archbishops in both hierarchies were designated by exactly the same territorial titles – Archbishop of Armagh, Archbishop of Tuam, Bishop of Meath etc. That duality was accepted then, as it is accepted today.

Cardinal Wiseman was nonetheless alarmed by what he read in *The Times*. He thereupon wrote to the Prime Minister, Lord John Russell, to explain that his title Archbishop of Westminster was 'purely ecclesiastical' and did not imply that he claimed any secular or territorial power. He was not to know that Russell had already made up his mind and had written what would be described as 'the most famous assault on English Catholicism in the nineteenth century'. That famous assault was the letter Russell sent to Edward Maltby, Bishop of Durham. The 'Durham Letter', as that document has since been called, was in reply to Bishop Maltby's complaints about 'the nature of the Papal Aggression'. In it Russell agreed that there was

> an assumption of power in all the documents that have come from Rome; a pretension of supremacy over the realm of England, and a claim to sole and undivided sway, which is inconsistent with the Queen's supremacy, with the rights of our bishops and clergy, and with the spiritual independence of the nation.

Though accused, when he published the Durham Letter, of encouraging religious intolerance, Russell proceeded with the parliamentary bill that in August 1851 became the much disputed Ecclesiastical Titles Act. Under that act anyone assuming unauthorised titles such as bishop or archbishop of 'pretended sees in the United Kingdom' would be fined £100. That, of course, was merely a reaffirmation of the penalty imposed in 1829 for the same offence. The act also declared that anyone introducing 'Papal Bills, Briefs, Rescripts or Letters' into the United Kingdom would also be fined £100. Previously the penalty for that offence was death.

The Ecclesiastical Titles Act was repealed in 1871. During the twenty years between enactment and repeal the act was considered by some to be little more than an inconvenience, and by others a denial of religious rights. But there were those who regarded the act as a necessary defence of the Protestant Establishment. In 1868 the House of Lords declared it 'a timely statement of the Royal Supremacy', the Monarch having been, since the time of King Henry the Eighth, Supreme Governor of the Church of England.

* * *

At 63 years of age Montgomery and Cooke would have been

considered quite elderly in 1851. In those times, when many common diseases that can easily be treated or prevented today were still incurable, a great many people died in middle age or earlier. Two of Cooke's sons were still youths when they died. One of his daughters died a young adult. Five of Montgomery's ten children died young. There were of course some people, here and there, who lived exceptionally long lives. Sir Moses Montefiore, the most active British Zionist of the nineteenth century, celebrated his 100th birthday in 1884. Montgomery's sister-in-law, widow of a Belfast man called George Ash, died at the age of 99. Prime Minister Gladstone was in his 90th year when he died. But people of such advanced age were exceptions.

In 1851 Montgomery and Cooke had still many years to live but as they grew older they became understandably less and less active. Montgomery suffered much from the long-term after-effects of rheumatic fever. He endured the excruciating pain of renal calculus. After the ownership of the dissenters' chapels was settled, he returned to attend full-time to the affairs of his congregation and to farm the glebe at Dunmurry. He had retired from his teaching post in the Belfast Academical Institution in 1837 but continued for the rest of his life to teach a small number of private pupils. Like most other Christian ministers he preached charity sermons when requested. He was active in famine relief during the years of the great catastrophe and would occasionally speak at election meetings in support of candidates of his own liberal outlook.

When the tenant farmers, many of them of the Presbyterian community in Ulster, were endeavouring to have their merely customary rights and safeguards made safe and permanent in law, Montgomery supported the Tenant Rights Movement and the League of the North and South.

Henry Cooke did not oppose tenant right when it was mentioned at meetings of the General Assembly, but generally he was not enthusiastic. He had too many close friends among the landowners. At a presentation in Belfast on 6 July 1865, the Marquis of Downshire praised him as one who had always impressed on the intelligent people of Ulster that the landed proprietors and their industrious tenants had a common interest in the conscientious discharge of their mutual obligations.

The presentation that day was in honour of Cooke himself. He received a cheque for £1,680 in recognition of his conspicuous pre-eminence throughout the British Empire as 'a distinguished and successful champion of Protestantism'.

In matters of politics and religion, even in his old age, Cooke continued to be the more controversial figure. During a serious outbreak of sectarian violence in Belfast in the summer of 1857 he upheld the right of sectarian clergymen, such as Hugh Hanna, to preach open-air sermons in which they demonised the Catholic clergy and slandered the local Catholic community. The Presbyterian's weekly newspaper, *Banner of Ulster*, published a statement in which he accused the Catholics of trying to stop the preaching of the Christian gospel.

> Allow them to stop our preaching in the streets [he declared] and they will soon stop it in the churches.

He changed his mind, however, when he saw that the civic authorities, Robert B Knox, the Protestant Bishop of Down and Conor, and most of the Presbyterian clergy wanted an end to open-air sectarian sermons.

In 1862 Cooke, Moderator that year of the General Assembly of the Presbyterian Church, was one of the speakers at 'a great Protestant meeting' in the Belfast Botanic Gardens. Porter, who mentions that event in his biography of Cooke, does not say what the meeting in the Botanic Gardens was about. It was in fact an Orange demonstration against the Party Processions Act which banned Orange parades and all other potentially dangerous displays of sectarianism. Cooke was at the Botanic Gardens, supporting what the Orangemen considered their right to march, at a time when by far the greater number of Presbyterian ministers would have nothing whatever to do with the Orange Order and when indeed eminent Orangemen such as Thomas Drew, the Vicar of Christ Church in Belfast, thought that because of their more liberal political outlook Presbyterians were not the sort of people who would be welcome in an Orange lodge.

Cooke's last appearance on a political platform was in October 1867. On that occasion he returned to Hillsborough to speak at a demonstration against what Porter described as

the attacks then being vigorously commenced against the Protestant institutions and endowments of Ireland.

What Porter meant was that the government and an increasing number of MPs were by then convinced that the Church of Ireland should be disestablished and left to make its own way as a Christian institution.

Robert B Knox was one of the few Protestant churchmen who knew and acknowledged that disestablishment was inevitable, and probably desirable. He therefore would have nothing to do with this second Hillsborough demonstration. He was accused of being unfaithful to the church in which he was a 'representative bishop' when he refused to postpone the diocesan conference that year so that certain of his clergy could be at Hillsborough.

Thomas Macknight, editor of the *Northern Whig*, went to Hillsborough and came back to report that the demonstration was a total failure. He noted that although the organisers had done everything possible to attract a large crowd there were not more than 4,000 people at the rally. There were perhaps another 2,000 loitering in the local pubs but not in the least interested in the speakers or the distinguished gentlemen on the platform. J L Porter, who was also at Hillsborough that day, claimed that 'thirty thousand people were present'. Macknight was a Liberal, Porter a Conservative. Maybe that accounts for the difference between four thousand and thirty thousand.

At seventy-nine years of age Henry Cooke was no longer the impressive orator he had been in earlier years. Macknight saw him at Hillsborough as 'a man bending under the weight of his years', his eyes filled with tears, trembling all over as he was helped on to the platform. His long hair and his long beard were 'white as the snow drift'. It was a sad sight, wrote J L Porter, the great orator, the great political leader, the great Protestant chieftain now with feeble voice and trembling lips trying to address a few parting words.

Cooke's speech was an indistinct mutter even to those near enough to hear him. He apologised for his age and his frailty but not for his prejudices.

> ... the snows of eighty years are upon my brow and the progress of the years has taken away my voice and, as you see, diminished my strength. The only change that has not come over me is a change in my views; my heart is unchanged. It is Protestant – universal to the core.

Macknight noted that a short time after Cooke had finished his brief speech and had sat down he was 'carried from the platform and through the crowd in an exhausted and helpless state'.

Cooke's last political declaration was issued on 24 October 1868 during a general election. His principal concern was that the Church of Ireland would be disestablished and disendowed if the Liberals (the Whigs) were returned with a majority but he told those electors to whom his appeal was addressed that all the Protestant churches were under threat, not just the Church of Ireland. The overthrow of the churches was the policy of the Liberals. The Conservatives were the only reliable defenders of the nation's religion. The election was therefore a contest in which no one could be neutral. Protestants should be ever faithful to their country and their religion, watchful always against 'the insidious advances of Popish error and despotism', and united 'in defence of liberty and truth'.

The Church of Ireland was disestablished by Act of Parliament in the summer of 1869. Cooke was dead by then. He died peacefully in his own bedroom, in his own house in South Belfast, at five o'clock on the evening of Sunday 13 December 1868. His surviving children, one son and three daughters, and the domestic staff were the only people present. His wife had died, after a short and sudden illness, the previous June.

Cooke had expressed the wish that there be no display of public grief on the day of his funeral. His request was that the mourners be limited to members of his own family, a few close friends in the Presbyterian ministry, one person representing the congregation of May Street Church, one layman to represent the Church of Ireland, and Alderman John Lytle from the Corporation of Belfast. But that was not how it was. Belfast Town Hall was 'crowded to excess' when in response to 'a requisition signed by the leading gentry and merchants', the mayor convened a meeting

> for the purpose of considering the propriety of having a public funeral for the interment of the remains of the late Rev Henry Cooke, DD, LL D as a mark of public respect and esteem for his memory.

A resolution to the same effect was moved by the Protestant Bishop of Down and Conor and seconded by the Orange politician William Johnston MP. A committee to arrange the public funeral was then appointed. And despite Cooke's last wishes the family consented to whatever arrangements might be made for an imposing public funeral.

By noon on Friday 18 December the crowds had gathered in the vicinity of the Cooke residence, beside the Ormeau Park. The procession was organised by Rev William Johnston, Minister of Townsend Street Presbyterian Church. He was assisted by Head-Constable Rankin, Police Commissioner Bailey, Sub-Inspector Harvey, and the men of the Royal Irish Constabulary.

The ministers of the Presbyterian General Assembly led the procession, followed by the hearse. The staff and students of Assembly's College, of which Cooke had been president, of Queen's College and of Magee College were dressed in their distinctive academic robes. Clergy and laymen of the Wesleyan, Baptist, and Unitarian churches followed. The private carriage of Dr Patrick Dorrian, Catholic Bishop of Down and Conor, was in the rear, among the equipage of the nobility and the influential rich.

But did Bishop Dorrian actually attend the funeral of Henry Cooke? According to J L Porter the bishop was indeed there.

Then came the mourning coaches and the long line of 154 carriages of the nobility and gentry, that of Dr Dorrian, the Roman Catholic Bishop, being among the number.

But Ambrose Macauley, who has written a biography of Bishop Dorrian, suggests that the bishop had his doubts, even though Cooke himself had been one of the mourners at the funeral of Cornelius Denvir, the former Catholic bishop, two years earlier. Dorrian felt that the public funeral was a carefully-planned 'tribute to Cooke's public life'. All who attended would, therefore, be endorsing Henry Cooke's 'public acts and labours'. That, he said, was something that he in clear conscience could not do.

Cooke was buried in Malone Cemetery which was then two miles outside Belfast.

The very next day, Saturday 19 December, there was another public meeting, this time to decide 'an appropriate form of memorial' to Henry Cooke. That memorial is, of course, the statue that stands to this day at the junction of Wellington Place and College Square East. It rises nine feet high and stands on a fifteen-foot pedestal. The statue of the young Earl of Belfast, which had stood on the site since 1855, was removed and re-erected inside the Town Hall in order to make room for that massive image of Henry Cooke*.

There was no public ceremony when the Cooke statue was unveiled in March 1876. The authorities feared some sort of violent sectarian protest. Belfast was already internationally notorious, in the middle years of the nineteenth century, as a place of sectarian unrest and ghetto riots.

There may have been no public ceremony at the unveiling in March but there was a demonstration, not hostile but nonetheless sectarian, two months later. In his book, *Belfast's Original Black Man*, the late Brendan Colgan describes 'a huge Orange rally ... a living mass of people extending in all directions' at the Cooke statue on 11 May 1876.

* * *

*Brendan Colgan, *Belfast's Original Black Man* (Belfast 1994)

Henry Montgomery had passed away in December 1865, three years before Cooke. In his later years he could see that the private judgement which he once defended with much energy and eloquence must always end in division and disagreement. Within the Remonstrant Synod of Ulster private judgement became a form of 'radical Unitarianism', especially among those younger ministers who were influenced at the time by the publications and opinions of two Americans, Theodore Parker and Ralph Waldo Emerson.

Parker and Emerson were Unitarian ministers, and free-thinkers in matters of religion. They wrote. They lectured. They travelled in Europe and America. Emerson particularly believed that each man must be 'the supreme judge for himself in spiritual matters'. They both therefore

> called in question the supernatural origins of Christianity and laid great stress on biblical criticism.

Montgomery was shocked and saddened at what he must have thought this new and outrageous interpretation of the Word of God. He reminded the 'young radicals' that there was a limit beyond which Christian liberty could not go. Christians, he said, could act only within the context of the gospel. Any form of liberty beyond that might be rational or philosophical but it would not be Christian. He consequently revised the Remonstrant Synod's Code of Discipline to include

> certain theological questions [that would] be put to candidates for the ministry in order to satisfy Presbyteries that candidates believed in the Divine origins and authority of Christianity.

Several congregations protested against that revision of the code, and left the Remonstrant Synod. The Presbytery of Antrim was divided into those who agreed with Montgomery and those who disagreed. The controversy lasted until the death of Montgomery and continued for years afterwards. It created havoc among the Irish Non-Subscribing Presbyterians, almost destroying their image and certainly weakening the influence they could have had.

Today, in the early years of the twenty-first century, the Non-Subscribing Presbyterian Church in Ireland consists of about 3,500 members in 33 congregations, divided into three presbyteries. There is a congregation in Dublin and one in Cork. But nowadays Unitarianism does not define any particular doctrine. It is more a general term for whatever theology individual Non-Subscribing Presbyterians might accept. Today the Non-Subscribing Presbyterian Church 'remains aloof from any definitive theological stance, whether Trinitarian, Unitarian or whatever'.

From that it would seem that it is the libertarianism of Emerson and Parker that has prevailed, not the theology of Arius, Socinus, or Henry Montgomery.

John A Crozier never wrote the second volume of his biography of Montgomery but he did write an informative 16-page pamphlet, *Henry Montgomery LL D.* which was published by the Ulster Unitarian Christian Association in 1888. Many years later Rev William McMillan, Minister of the Non-Subscribing Presbyterian Church in Newry, published *A Profile in Courage*, the text of the lecture on the life of Henry Montgomery which was delivered in the church at Dunmurry on Sunday 27 March 1966.

J L Porter claimed that Henry Cooke's whole life was devoted to 'pure religion, sound education, and constitutional government'. He was therefore 'held high in the esteem and affectation of the nation'. But not everyone who knew Cooke would have agreed and certainly not everyone in the Presbyterian community. There were many Presbyterians, as well as others, who, like Sir James Graham, regarded him as an intolerant and narrow-minded man. And there were orthodox Presbyterian congregations who would not have him anywhere near them. Isaac Nelson, minister of a congregation in West Belfast, said in 1867 that Cooke had been 'talking about the Bible for nearly sixty years without throwing any light on its contents'.*

Nelson also predicted riots and recurring riots in Belfast if

---

*Quoted by R Finlay Holmes in *Henry Cooke*

the sectarian incitements of men like Cooke and Hugh Hanna were not curbed and controlled. Others were, of course, of a different opinion. In May 1888 the Presbyterians published a selection of

Commemorative Addresses
illustrative of the life, character, and
distinguished public services of
The Rev Henry Cooke DD, LLD
on the centenary of his birth, 11th May 1888

Hugh Hanna, who had been named often in official and unofficial reports as an agitator who incited sectarian disorder, was a member of the committee that organised the commemoration but he was only one of the supporting speakers.

The principal speaker was Professor T H Witherow. He was eloquent and reasonable when he explained why orthodox Presbyterian feared that if the Unitarians (the Arians) had been tolerated much longer they would have undermined the Presbyterian Church in Ireland. That, at least, is what he feared would have happened

if Dr Cooke, at so great a cost of toil and trouble, had not stood in the breach, or had made the attempt and failed.

Witherow then explained how Arianism had destroyed the Presbyterian Church in England and how it became the dominant and ineradicable influence in the Dutch Reformed Church. But he also admitted that as 'a consistent Conservative' Cooke differed politically from most of his brethren, whether orthodox or otherwise, in the Presbyterian ministry.

Perhaps it was too early, in May 1888, for Witherow, or anyone else, to notice that the traditionally Liberal political outlook of Irish Presbyterians was already undergoing a change that would soon be permanent. Gladstone's first attempt to grant the Irish people Home Rule in 1886 alarmed many Irish Liberals, whether Presbyterian or of any other church. They became Liberal Unionists and eventually joined with Conservatives of the same outlook to become Ulster Unionists. Hugh Hanna and a few others went further. They were already Ulster Unionists and in 1886 conspired to resist Home Rule, even to the extent of importing weapons and threatening rebellion. *Ulster will fight and Ulster will be right. Home Rule is Rome rule.* Those were the slogans and battle-cries of the Unionist rebels.

During the course of his commemorative address, Professor Witherow doubted if whoever might be presiding at the bicentenary of the birth of Henry Cooke one hundred years in the future would be able to say that among the Presbyterians of Ireland there had arisen

> a second man worthy in every respect to rank with that fine old Christian soldier [Henry Cooke], that Gideon of his generation.

Witherow was evidently saying that there was only one 'Henry Cooke'. There would be nobody else like him.

The bicentenary of the birth of Cooke was not publicly commemorated in May 1988, but twenty years earlier on 12/13 December 1968, which was the 100th anniversary of his death, the *Belfast Telegraph* had published two articles by John Barkley, the last of the Presbyterian radicals, Professor of Church History in the Assembly's College, Belfast.

Barkley was fair and generous in his comments, and considerate. He noted that to some people Cooke was still 'a saint from heaven' but to many others just 'a narrow-minded bigot'. Being himself an orthodox Presbyterian he accepted Cooke's determination to get rid of the Arians as theologically justified, even if he considered his methods ill-advised. But to him Cooke was, above all, 'a man of moral courage'.

It is often said, despite the understandable doubts expressed by Professor Witherow in 1888, that there actually is a 'Henry Cooke' in every generation of Ulster's Protestant theologians, and sometimes more than one. That is most certainly true, even down to the present day. All of them remain, however, nothing but vulgar imitations of the original Henry Cooke.

Sources

Akenson, D H: *The Irish Education Experiment*

Colgan, Brendan: *Belfast's Original Black Man* (Belfast 1994)

Crawford, Robert: *The Cooke Centenary* (Belfast 1888)

Crozier, J A: *The Life of the Rev Henry Montgomery LL D* (London 1875)

— *Henry Montgomery LL D* (Belfast 1888)

Guttsman, W L: *The British Political Elite* (London 1963)

Holmes, R Finlay: *Henry Cooke* (Belfast, Dublin, Ottawa 1981)

Macknight, Thos.: *Ulster As It Is* (London 1896)

McMillan, Rev Wm: *A Profile in Courage* (Newry 1966)

Norman, E R: *Anti-Catholicism in Victorian England* (London 1968)

Ó Tuathaigh, G.: *Ireland Before the Famine: 1798-1848* (Dublin 1972)

Porter, J L: *Life and Times of Henry Cooke DD LLD* (Belfast 1877)

Rogers, Patrick: *Ulster Presbyterianism and Irish Politics, 1798-1829* (The Capuchin Annual, Dublin 1943)

Seery, James, Holmes, Finlay & Stewart, ATQ: *Presbyterians, the United Irishmen and 1798* (Belfast 2000)

Swords, Liam (ed): *Protestant, Catholic & Dissenter: The Clergy and 1798* (Dublin 1997)

Belfast Literary Society 1801-1901: *Historical Sketch with Memoirs of Some Distinguished Members* (Belfast 1902)

— *The Repealer Repulsed* (Belfast 1841)